HOOP
HEROES

GREG GARBER

MetroBooks

MetroBooks

An imprint of Friedman/Fairfax Publishers

Library of Congress Cataloging-in-Publication Data

Garber, Angus G.
    Hoop heroes / by Greg Garber.
       p.   cm.
    Includes index.
    ISBN 1-56799-250-1
    1. Basketball players--United States--Biography.   2. National
Basketball Association.   I. Title.
GV884.A1G37   1996
796.323'092'2--dc20
[B]   95-35441
                                   CIP

Editors: Nathaniel Marunas and Stephen Slaybaugh
Art Director: Jeff Batzli
Designer: Kevin Ullrich
Photography Editor: Wendy Missan

Color separations by HK Scanner Arts Int'l Ltd.
Printed in Hong Kong and bound in China by Midas Printing Limited

For bulk purchases and special sales, please contact:
Friedman/Fairfax Publishers
Attention: Sales Department
15 West 26th Street
New York, NY 10010
212/685-6610 Fax 212/685-1307

Dedication

For Austin Michael Marrett, a boy with the genetic advantages and the resolve to be a future hoop hero.

Acknowledgments

Thanks to today's terrific young basketball players for their skill, their patience, and their time. Thanks also to: the Basketball Hall of Fame in Springfield, Massachusetts, especially Wayne R. Patterson in research; the public relations men of the National Basketball Association; and Steve Slaybaugh of the Michael Friedman Publishing Group.

Contents

Introduction

In the early 1990s, the National Basketball Association found itself looking for a few good men. Where had the heroes gone? Magic Johnson left the Los Angeles Lakers after the 1990–91 season when he announced he was HIV-positive. He did make a final, triumphant appearance in the 1992 All-Star Game, in which he scored 25 points in 29 minutes and was named the Most Valuable Player.

Larry Bird, who like Johnson entered the league in 1979, left the Boston Celtics after 1991–92 with a chronically aching back. Michael Jordan, who carried the Chicago Bulls to three straight league championships and won seven straight scoring titles, quit basketball after the 1992–93 season. He decided to play baseball for the Chicago White Sox organization instead. He would return on March 19, 1995, but by then he was thirty-two years old. Johnson. Bird. Jordan. They were the three greatest players of their generation, three of the best in history, and at the beginning of the 1993–94 season, they were no longer on the NBA stage. Where would the new talent come from? Who could possibly match the skill of Jordan, the competitiveness of Bird, or the smile of Johnson?

Shaquille O'Neal and Alonzo Mourning are examples of young stars helping to elevate today's game of basketball to another level.

Fortunately for the NBA and its many fans, the 1992, 1993, and 1994 college drafts provided an incredible supply of slams, jams, and, yes, even big-league smiles. Their names are Shaquille O'Neal, Grant Hill, Chris Webber, Anfernee Hardaway, Jason Kidd, Latrell Sprewell, Jimmy Jackson, and Glenn "Big Dog" Robinson. They represent perhaps the most exciting crop of newcomers to the league in recent memory.

Throw in a handful of established stars like Charles Barkley, Reggie Miller, David Robinson, and Hakeem Olajuwon, and you have a league that is full of excitement and promise.

And while new stars are emerging and new teams winning, it is important to remember the great teams and players from the past. Teams like the Los Angeles Lakers and the Boston Celtics have had long histories of winning. Players like Moses Malone and Wilt Chamberlain set records that may never be broken.

So, here are all of today's young guns (and a few older ones), with all kinds of important statistics: things like shoe sizes, favorite foods, contract details, and middle names, as well as the great teams of the past and the franchises to watch in the future.

Dr. James Naismith, a physical education teacher by trade, invented the game of basketball to keep his students occupied during the cold winter months.

Dr. James Naismith

Dr. James Naismith was a gym teacher, and he had a major problem on his hands: eighteen bored, restless students cooped up inside while the cold New England wind blew outside. And so, the physical education instructor at the School for Christian Workers in Springfield, Massachusetts, was forced to be creative. He invented basketball. The year was 1881.

Naismith asked the school janitor to attach boxes to the railings at opposite ends of the cramped gymnasium, but the janitor used peach baskets instead, nailing them 10 feet above the floor. Using positions from the Canadian game of lacrosse, Naismith instructed the nine players on each side to shoot a soccer ball at the goals. He also posted thirteen rules for his new game on the gym door. Running with the ball, holding, pushing, and tripping were all forbidden. The team with the most goals after two 15-minute halves was the winner.

The game filled a void. The students were no longer bored and the game quickly became popular. In February 1881, the first public game pitted students against teachers: the students won, 5–1. By the end of the year, the game had spread through the YMCA network to places like Pennsylvania and Iowa.

"The more I watch the game, the more I realize that while easy to understand and simple to demonstrate, it is nevertheless a challenge to skill," Dr. Naismith wrote in 1939. "It is only through grounding in the fundamentals and constant practice that championships are won. Just how many persons engage in the game of basketball, no one knows, but the number must be large."

Today, of course, the game is huge in just about every country all around the world.

Sir Charles
Charles Barkley

Charles Wade Barkley was a terrific college player at Auburn; he actually broke the school record for blocked shots midway through his sophomore season. But people wondered if he was big enough and strong enough at six feet six inches (198 cm) and 252 pounds (114 kg) to excel at the power forward position in the NBA. Bobby Knight, the coach of the United States Olympic Basketball Team in 1984, was one of them. Barkley did not make Knight's final roster, but the Philadelphia 76ers were willing to take a chance on him.

The 76ers made Barkley the fifth player taken in the 1984 draft, and he quickly blossomed into an all-star. He was strong but, more importantly, astonishingly quick. He could grab a rebound on the defensive end, then dribble the length of the court and finish his own fast break with a layup. Sir Charles made the NBA All-Rookie team in 1985, averaging 14 points and 8.6 rebounds. His aggressive attitude and extreme confidence allowed him to outplay many taller and heavier opponents. Maybe it was something he learned from the two women who raised him: his mother, Charcey Glenn, and grandmother, Johnnie Mae Mickens.

As his career progressed, Barkley's signature became the offensive rebound. He collected league-high totals of 390 in 1986–87, 385 in 1987–88, and 403 in 1988–89. In one incredible burst, Barkley set an NBA record with 11 offensive rebounds in a single, 12-minute quarter against the New York Knicks in 1987.

At the same time, Barkley had a nifty scoring touch around the basket. Through ten NBA seasons, he averaged 23.3 points per game to go with 11.6 rebounds. One thing consistently overlooked about Barkley's game is his excellent shot selection. Barkley ranks second among active players in field goal percentage, with .562.

In 1992 the Phoenix Suns traded for Barkley in an attempt to win the NBA championship. They sent Jeff Hornacek, Andrew Lang, and Tim Perry to Philadelphia in exchange for Barkley. In

Below: Charles Barkley, here backing in on ex–world champion Bull Horace Grant, is one of the game's most versatile players. Opposite: Barkley can match muscle with taller, heavier power forwards like Grant, as well as dribble coast-to-coast with the ease of a point guard and slam the ball home.

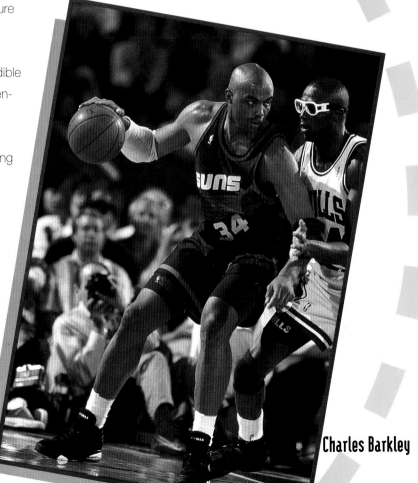

1993, he rewarded the Suns with a Most Valuable Player season of 25.6 points and 12.2 rebounds per game, but Phoenix fell just short in the playoffs. The next season, Barkley averaged 23 points per game and, despite talk of retirement, was expected to return for another year.

Looking back, Barkley doesn't have any regrets. Well, just one: "The one thing that really disturbed me is I never graduated from high school on time," said Barkley, a member of the NBA's All-Interview team. "I never got to be in that march or throw my hat in the air. That has always bothered me. But you know what? It was my own fault."

In 1992, Barkley made up for his Olympic disappointment eight years earlier. As a member of the Dream Team, he won a gold medal in Barcelona, Spain.

During the 1994–95 season, he claimed it would be his last. "My first goal in 1996 is to relax," he said. "And that means playing a lot of golf. After that, I'll consider a career in politics, but not television commentary like a lot of people think. TV is hard work and, hey, I don't want to work that hard."

> **"I don't care who's the best player, I just want to be the richest one. They can argue who's the best, but I'll be set for life."**
> **—Charles Barkley**

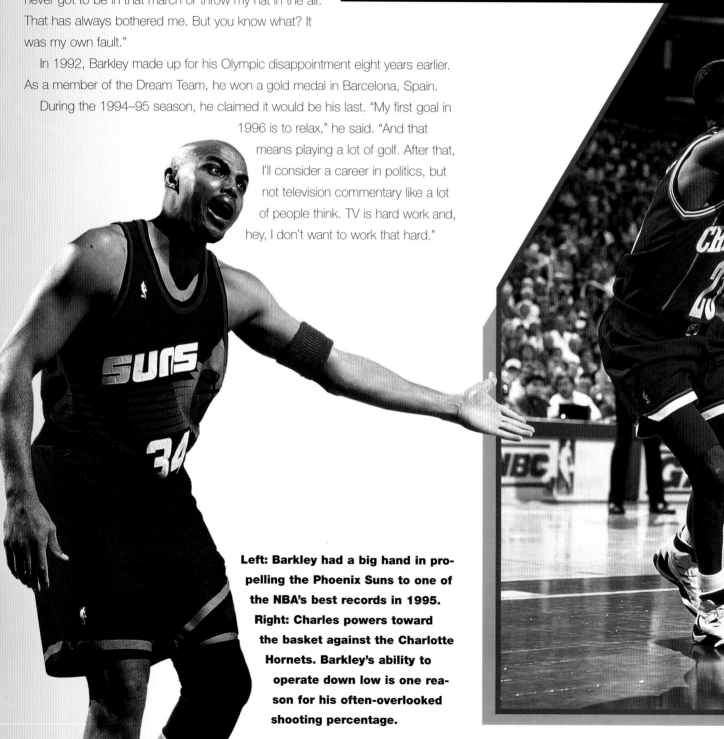

Left: Barkley had a big hand in propelling the Phoenix Suns to one of the NBA's best records in 1995. Right: Charles powers toward the basket against the Charlotte Hornets. Barkley's ability to operate down low is one reason for his often-overlooked shooting percentage.

The First Game

There was a time—the 1930s and 1940s—when college basketball was all the rage. In fact, the professional game was practically nonexistent, something that promoter Ned Irish was intent on changing.

In 1946, Irish began putting together something he called the Basketball Association of America (BAA). There would be eleven teams: Washington, Philadelphia, New York, Providence, Toronto, Boston, Chicago, St. Louis, Cleveland, Detroit, and Pittsburgh. The first game, between the New York Knicks and the Toronto Huskies, was scheduled for November 1 at Maple Leaf Gardens.

The posters around Toronto urged fans to come see the "jet propelled" Huskies play "big-league basketball, the world's most popular sport," featuring "thrills, spills, action, and speed." Tickets were priced at 75 cents, $1.25, $2.00, and $2.50.

A total of 7,090 curious fans showed up to witness a piece of history. Ossie Schectman of the Knicks scored the new league's first points on a driving layup. Schectman had played for the legendary Clair Bee at Long Island University and helped the Blackbirds to National Invitational Tournament victories in 1939 and 1941. The Knicks went on to win the opener, 68–66.

Ultimately, the Washington Capitols posted the best regular-season record, 49–11. But Philadelphia prevailed over Chicago in the finals to win the first championship.

From that modest beginning, the BAA soon blossomed into the National Basketball Association.

Muggsy
Tyrone Bogues

Okay, you are five feet three inches (160 cm). That was all you could manage on the height chart at the doctor's office after high school. And now you want to be a player in a major college program and, later, in the National Basketball Association. That's right, you're 63 inches (160 cm) tall in a world of skyscrapers. So what do you do?

If you are Tyrone "Muggsy" Bogues, you play the same point guard game you've always played—a cutting, slashing game predicated on speed and savvy. If you are Muggsy Bogues, all 144 pounds (65 kg) of him, you become a success at every level. Against all odds, it's true. You can look it up.

Even in high school, Bogues ran with a fast crowd. He played for Dunbar High School in Baltimore, the team that went undefeated and won the national championship during his senior season, 1983. Also on that team were future NBA first-round draft picks Reggie Lewis and Reggie Williams, as well as future Hornet teammate David Wingate. Bogues, by the way, was the Most Valuable Player of that high school team of stars.

After four years at Wake Forest in North Carolina, Bogues had yet to prove he didn't belong. In fact, he finished as the Atlantic Coast Conference's all-time leader in assists (781) and steals (275). In his junior season, Bogues averaged 11.3 points, 8.4 assists, and 3.1 steals per game. As a senior, he led the Demon Deacons in scoring with 14.8 points a game and somehow wound up with 3.8 rebounds per game, second among guards in the ACC.

The Washington Bullets made Bogues the twelfth pick of the 1987 draft and he had a solid rookie season. He produced 404 assists, 393 points, 136 rebounds, 127 steals, and 3 blocked shots. The Charlotte Hornets liked what they saw and scooped him up in the expansion draft of 1988.

Bogues has become an institution in Charlotte, North Carolina, where his scoring touch has improved virtually every season. His 1993–94 season was his best overall as a professional. Bogues averaged 10.8 points per game, as well as 10.1 assists, second in the NBA. In 1994–95, Bogues averaged 11.1 points

Below: With Muggsy Bogues passing to Larry Johnson, the Charlotte Hornets are one of the league's rising teams. Opposite: Bogues' ability to handle the ball in a game dominated by big men is consistently amazing.

Manute Bol

He stood a rather spindly seven feet seven inches (231 cm), but Manute Bol had great determination. Born a member of the Dinka tribe in Gogrial, Sudan, Bol played soccer and handball growing up. He emerged at the University of Bridgeport Connecticut during the 1984–85 season, producing an average of 22.5 points, 13.5 rebounds, and 7 blocked shots per games. His slight build—he weighed only 225 pounds (102 kg)—worked against him in the professional ranks.

The Washington Bullets saw him as a defensive specialist and chose him in the second round of the 1985 draft. In a game against Atlanta, Bol blocked an amazing 17 shots. He finished the 1985–86 season with 397 blocks, the second-highest rookie total in National Basketball Association history.

Bol never scored a lot of points, but he enjoyed a productive career in the NBA, moving to Golden State for two seasons, then to Philadelphia.

and 8.7 assists per game. It was the seventh consecutive season he led the Hornet assists, dishing off the ball to the likes of Larry Johnson and Alonzo Mourning.

Bogues lives in Charlotte and spends most of his free time with his wife, Kimberly their daughters, Tyeisha and Brittany, and son, Tyrone Jr. His favorite sports, other th ketball, are softball and golf. One of his biggest off-season interests is summer bask camps for kids. They have always responded to him well, perhaps because he seer one of them.

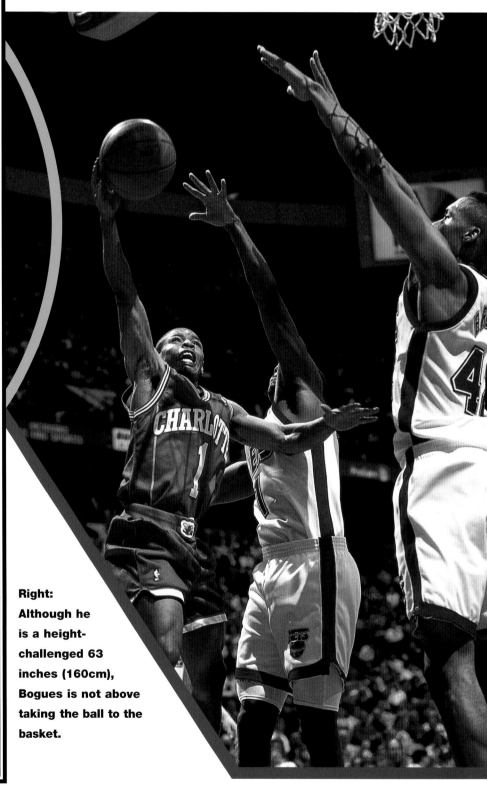

Right: Although he is a height-challenged 63 inches (160cm), Bogues is not above taking the ball to the basket.

The Three-Point Shot

Being tall is not a prerequisite in basketball, but it sure helps. It's a matter of mathematics: the closer you are to the basket, the easier it is to score–in theory, anyway.

Well, the National Basketball Association made a radical rule change before the 1979–80 season by allowing a three-point shot. The trey had been popular in the American Basketball Association, and the NBA was looking for something to create a little drama away from the basket. The line was drawn twenty-three feet and nine inches (7.2m) away from the basket at its farthest point and a more manageable twenty-two feet (6.7m) from the baseline corners.

The principle was simple: create an incentive (an extra point) for the outside shot and open up the game. The three-point shot had a noticeable effect on NBA defenses. The subtle (and illegal) zones were forced to stretch away from the basket, relieving congestion in the lane that the wide-bodies were causing. After all, when James Naismith invented the game of basketball more than a century ago, he didn't envision a handful of seven-foot (213 cm) players battling under the basket.

The experiment worked. The smaller player was suddenly operating on a level field. Consider the numbers: when Los Angeles Lakers center Kareem Abdul-Jabbar cruised in for a slam dunk at close range, he received 2 points. When Lakers guard Norm Nixon swished a twenty-four-foot (7.3m) basket from outside, a far tougher shot, he received 3 points.

The laws of probability make the three-point shot in the hands of an expert a sound choice. While a good

No one has ever hit more three-point baskets in a single season than Dan Majerle of the Phoenix Suns.

shooter in the NBA makes half his shots, the best three-point artists are good for 40 percent of their shots. So if Jabbar made 5 of 10 shots, he received 10 points. If Nixon made 4 of 10 shots, he received 12 points.

Not surprisingly, the best three-point shooters are generally sharp-eyed, sure-handed guards. The five career leaders in shooting percentage are Steve Kerr (.445), B.J. Armstrong (.443), the late Drazen Petrovic (.437), Mark Price (.409), and Trent Tucker (.408).

The exception to the rule is swingman Dale Ellis. At six feet seven inches (200cm), Ellis can play both guard and forward, but his shot is silky and smooth from three-point range. In fact, heading into the 1994–95 season, Ellis had made an NBA-record 1,013 three-point baskets wearing uniforms for Dallas, Seattle, Milwaukee, and San Antonio.

More three-point facts: Dan Majerle of Phoenix holds the single-season record, with 192. Scott Wedman of the Boston Celtics hit 11 straight treys over a three-month period in the 1984–85 season. On April 8, 1993, Miami's Brian Shaw knocked down an amazing 10 three-pointers. Michael Adams, then of Denver, made three-pointers in 46 consecutive games in 1988. Five players have led the league in treys twice: Darrell Griffith, Larry Bird, Vernon Maxwell, Adams, and Majerle. In an attempt to further open up the game, the NBA changed the three-point line for the 1994–95 season. Now, the arc is a consistent twenty-two feet (6.7m) from the basket all the way around, making the three-pointer a vital part of the game.

Ewing
Patrick Ewing

He stands a prototypical seven feet (213 cm) and weighs a sculptured 255 pounds (115 kg). He is a giant among the game's giants, but center Patrick Aloysius Ewing has worked hard to dominate every level at which he's played. Very hard. You can see it in the scowl he wears on the court for every game.

Consider that Ewing was born in Kingston, Jamaica, and moved to the United States with his parents when he was eleven. Consider that he played his high school ball at Cambridge Rindge & Latin in Massachusetts, hardly an athletic-sounding school, and became the unanimous choice as the national Player of the Year. Consider his career at Georgetown University: Ewing carried the Hoyas to three National Collegiate Athletic Association finals in four years, including the 1984 championship. Although he finished as the leading rebounder (1,316) and shot blocker (493) in school history, the purists complained that he was not a complete player. His four years at Georgetown produced only a 15.3-point scoring average.

When the New York Knicks made him the first choice in the 1985 draft, they gave him an amazing salary for those days: $30 million for ten seasons. Despite frequent injuries as a rookie and the tendency to commit silly fouls and despite being saddled with a coach who insisted on playing him out of position at power forward, Ewing was the NBA's Rookie of the Year. He averaged 20 points and 9 rebounds a game. And then he really took off.

Ewing's coming-out party was the first round of the playoffs in 1990. He personally dismissed the Boston Celtics and their Hall of Fame lineup, which included Larry Bird, Kevin McHale, and Robert Parish. Magic Johnson of the Los Angeles Lakers noticed the difference. "I've never seen him like this before,"

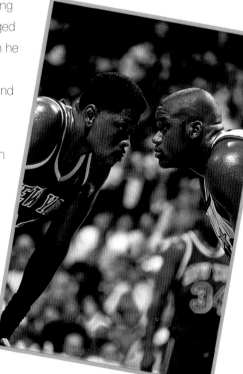

Patrick Ewing of the New York Knicks remains one of the giants of the game. Left: Ewing soars through the Indiana Pacers defense. Right: Staring down Shaquille O'Neal of the Orlando Magic.

Over the years, Ewing has developed an enviable versatility. In fact, his teammates sometimes wish he would pass up the eighteen-foot (5.4m) jump shot and take the ball inside, as he does here against the Los Angeles Clippers.

Johnson said. "Now he's learning to do it all inside and outside. His turn-around jump shot is deadly and when he gets inside the paint, he's got a very pretty hook shot. What I see, though, most of all, is tenaciousness. Now he is very, very active." Said Ewing, "Everybody keeps telling me how surprised they are with what I've done. But I'm telling you honestly that it doesn't surprise me. I knew I could do it."

And then he continued to do it, again and again. He has been to nine All-Star Games in ten seasons and has averaged more than 10 rebounds and 23 points a game as a professional. So much for shabby offensive skills. In 1993–94, Ewing carried the Knickerbockers all the way to the seventh game of the NBA finals before losing to the Houston Rockets.

"There are times when I feel unstoppable," Ewing said. "I'm confident, very confident. I've always been confident in myself. It's not ego-tripping or anything. I just know what I can do. I know how good I can be."

Wilt Chamberlain Scores 100

These days, when a National Basketball Association player really lights it up, he scores 40 points in a game. Today's stars are capable of more when they're at their best; Michael Jordan torched Cleveland for 69 points in 1990 and David Robinson poured in 71 in 1994 against the Los Angeles Clippers.

Believe it or not, those games pale in comparison to the night Wilt Chamberlain scored 100 points against the New York Knicks. It was March 2, 1962, and the seven-foot-one-inch (215cm) center of the Philadelphia Warriors had the game of a career before 4,124 fans in the Hersheypark Arena in Hershey, Pennsylvania.

Chamberlain scored 23 points in the first quarter and 18 in the second for 41 at the half. He added another 28 in the third quarter. That was when the quest for 100 really began. Chamberlain took 21 shots in the last quarter, making 12, and was 7 for 10 from the free throw line. On offense, the Knicks tried to run the clock down to prevent Chamberlain from reaching the century mark. On defense, all five Knicks players would surround him. Nothing seemed to work.

In the end, Chamberlain made 36 of 63 shots and 28 of 32 free throws, along with 25 rebounds. He smashed the previous record for points in a single NBA regular-season game, his own of 78, set earlier in the same season against Los Angeles. In fact, the four highest-scoring games on record belong to the Big Dipper. Chamberlain scored 73 twice in 1962, a total matched in 1978 by Denver's David Thompson.

In that 1961–62 season, Chamberlain averaged an astounding 50.4 points per game and scored a total of 4,029 points—both all-time records.

This is the actual basket that netted Wilt Chamberlain his 100th point against the New York Knicks on March 3, 1962, in Hershey, Pennsylvania.

Penny

Anfernee Hardaway

They call him Penny, but Anfernee Deon Hardaway's financial value to the Orlando Magic is impossible to calculate. Take the game he played against the Chicago Bulls on February 26, 1995, as an example. The Magic were without the NBA's most powerful player, center Shaquille O'Neal, who was serving a one-game suspension. Power forward Horace Grant, who had back spasms, also missed the game, and forward Donald Royal left in the first quarter with a sprained ankle. That left it up to Hardaway.

The six-foot-seven-inch (200 cm), 195-pound (8.5 kg) point guard, often lost in the wake of O'Neal, had the game of his young career. He scored 39 points, the last 2 on a monster breakaway dunk with less than one second left to give Orlando a breathtaking 105–103 victory over the Bulls. To people who have watched Hardaway emerge as one of the league's most exciting players, the result was hardly a surprise.

Yes, Hardaway is that good. For much of his basketball life, he has been compared with Magic Johnson, a tough legacy to follow. Hardaway played three seasons at Memphis State, averaging 20 points per game and setting a school single-season scoring record as a junior.

On draft day in 1993, the Magic selected Michigan's Chris Webber with the first overall pick, then turned around and dealt the rights to Webber in exchange for first-round draft picks in the years 1996, 1998, and 2000, plus Hardaway, who had been the third overall choice of the Golden State Warriors. After signing a nine-year, $70 million contract, he played an impressive rookie season, averaging 16 points and 6.6 assists per game. Hardaway came within six votes of winning Rookie of the Year. That honor, oddly enough, went to Webber in the closest balloting in thirteen years.

For the first half of Hardaway's rookie season, the Magic used Scott Skiles as the point guard. But as the season progressed, so did Hardaway. His court vision grew and his spectacular no-look passes began to draw attention. He also became more confident around the basket and his shooting percentage increased dramatically. He was the only league rookie to start all 82 games. He ranked sixth overall in steals with 190, and broke Nick Anderson's team record for steals in the Magic's fifty-third game of the season.

They Love This Game!

In 1995, while Major League Baseball struggled in the wake of a wrenching labor dispute, the National Basketball Association made a powerful case that watching basketball is rapidly becoming the national pastime.

During the 1994–95 season, exactly 18,516,484 fans attended the 1,107 regular-season NBA games, representing a 2.96 percent increase from the previous record of 17,984,014, set the season before. It was the tenth time in the past twelve seasons that the league set a single-season attendance mark.

The average attendance of 16,727 fans per game was also an all-time record. NBA arenas around the country were filled to a record average of 93.6 percent capacity.

Inset: Hardaway was a consistent breakaway threat in the 1995 NBA Championship Finals against the Houston Rockets. Left: Hardaway's slashing power, evident in this soaring drive against the New Jersey Nets, is his trademark.

Anfernee Hardaway   23

The Highest-Scoring Game Ever

The Denver Nuggets, under coach Doug Moe, never met a shot they didn't like. Combine that lack of discipline with the trigger-happy Detroit Pistons, and throw in the thin air at Denver's McNichols Sports Arena the night of December 13, 1983, and you have a certifiable defensive disaster. To be specific: Denver and Detroit combined to score 370 points in a triple-overtime game, the most offensive game in the history of the National Basketball Association.

Clearly, the weapons were in place. Denver had forwards Alex English and Kiki Vandeweghe, who were in the process of becoming the first teammates to surpass 2,000 points each for two consecutive seasons. Detroit offered guard Isiah Thomas and forward Kelly Tripucka, who would both finish the regular season with 21.3-point scoring averages.

Detroit led 38–34 after the first quarter, but Denver came back to force a 74-each halftime tie. The Nuggets crept away to a 5-point lead in the third quarter, but the Pistons evened the count at 145 at the end of regulation. The two teams matched scores in the first two overtimes (14 points, then 12) before Detroit held on for a 186–184 victory.

Thomas, who played 52 of the game's 63 minutes, was the star. He finished with a season-high 47 points and 17 assists. John Long, the Pistons' other guard, scored 41 points, while Tripucka added 35 points. For Denver, Vandeweghe (51 points) and English (47) both played 50 minutes and reached season-high totals.

Defensive purists were disappointed; the two teams combined to make 142 of 251 shots, a 57 percent success rate.

The Detroit Piston's John Long, here driving past Richard Anderson of the Denver Nuggets, scored 41 points, and he was only the game's fourth-leading scorer.

"Penny just exploded to the basket and, wham, it was over."
—Tree Rollins

By 1995, his second year, Hardaway, only twenty-three, was the starting point guard for the East in the NBA All-Star Game. Using an awesome arsenal of shots, he averaged 20.9 points per game, moving Tree Rollins, Orlando's backup center and assistant coach, to describe this recent dunk on Knicks center Patrick Ewing: "Patrick is seven feet [213 cm] and about 250 pounds [113 kg], and Penny is six-seven [200 cm] and skinny as a rail," Rollins said. "When Penny took off for the hoop, I thought Patrick would either get the block or flatten him. But Penny just exploded to the basket and, wham, it was over."

Fortunately for the Magic, Hardaway's career as the man who takes care of the ball and of O'Neal is just beginning.

While Shaquille O'Neal is seen as the player that drives the Orlando Magic, Hardaway is truly the team's pulse. Here, he beats two Houston Rockets to the basket.

Gentleman
Grant Hill

Grant Hill is not a typical in-your-face superstar. He is quiet. He is humble. He does not style in the manner of, say, Deion Sanders or even Shaquille O'Neal. Heck, his middle name is Henry.

No, Hill is all about class. He is all about doing things the right way. That is because Hill grew up with role models in sports. The first was his father, Calvin, who came out of Yale University and played running back for the Dallas Cowboys, Washington Redskins, and Cleveland Browns. Two others were tennis player Arthur Ashe and the wondrous Julius Erving.

"I was young when he was coming to the end of his career, but I remember being taken [with] Dr. J," Hill said. "The thing I liked best was that he carried himself with class. He never went out of his way to embarrass anybody. I feel like I come from a generation that has the wrong type of heroes.

"I never got to see Arthur Ashe play tennis, but I saw the way he lived his life after tennis. I always felt that he was the type of person I should be looking up to because of his spirit. It's a matter of respect."

This man who lives for respect happens to be a terrific basketball player, one whom people compare quite often with Michael Jordan. Hill is six foot eight inches (203 cm) and 225 pounds (101.2 kg), and, like Jordan, plays with an air of grace. His career at Duke reads like a storybook.

As a freshman for Coach Mike Krzyzewski's Blue Devils, Hill played more than 24 minutes a game, scoring an average of 11.2 points. Playing with Bobby Hurley and Christian Laettner, Hill helped Duke to the national championship that season. Duke repeated the following year; in all, Hill and the Blue Devils visited the finals three times in his four years.

Not only was Hill a great leader, but he excelled in every facet of the game. As a senior, Hill led Duke in scoring (17.4 points), assists (5.2), and steals (64), and was second in rebounding (6.9). He was also a tenacious defender who usually covered the

> **"I was young when he was coming to the end of his career, but I remember being taken [with] Dr. J."**
> **—Grant Hill**

Below: Off the court, Grant Hill is gracious and well-mannered. Opposite: On the court, he is a sportsman who isn't afraid to throw the ball down with authority.

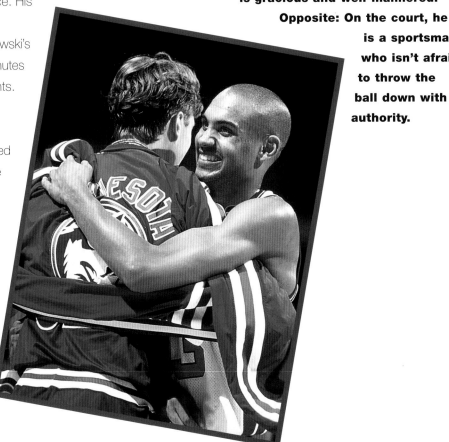

Right: Hill's size (six feet eight inches [203 cm]) does not prevent him from rebounding with the NBA's big men or maneuvering inside for layups and jams. Below: When Hill puts the ball on the floor, he has the quickness to leave the defenders in the wake.

opponent's best scorer. Not surprisingly, Hill was the first player in Atlantic Coast Conference history to produce more than 1,900 points, 700 rebounds, 400 assists, 200 steals, and 100 blocked shots.

The Detroit Pistons thought enough of his ability to make him the third player taken overall in the 1994 draft. It was their highest pick since 1981, when they made point guard Isiah Thomas the second overall choice. Detroit signed Hill to a $45 million guaranteed contract.

Hill made a rapid impression on the NBA and its fans. He was the leading vote-getter in the All-Star balloting and finished with 10 points in 20 All-Star minutes, making 5 of 8 shots. He averaged 19.9 points per game and shared the NBA's Rookie of the Year honors with Dallas guard Jason Kidd.

Bobby Hurley Returns

Bobby Hurley had one of the great college careers at Duke. He was the point guard for two national championship teams, in 1991 and 1992. He was drafted in the first round by the Sacramento Kings, but on December 12, 1993, the fairy tale ended.

Driving home from a Kings game in Sacramento, Hurley's car was struck by a station wagon. Hurley was thrown one hundred feet (30.4m) into a ditch. After he was pulled from a shallow pool of water, doctors discovered two collapsed lungs, a broken shoulder blade, a compression fracture of the back, torn ligaments in his knee, and a sprained wrist. Against all odds, Hurley lived.

"The condition I was in in the ditch," Hurley said, "the doctors have told me a lot of people wouldn't have made it to the hospital. There were a lot of coincidences that really helped me that night.

"It was a dark road, so I was lucky that someone was there to find me. Getting to the hospital, where just a week before the doctor on call was reading an article about an injury I had, his being able to diagnose it quickly and repair it.

"I was so scared that I wasn't going to live that the actual thought of whether I was going to play ball again never came into my mind."

As it turned out, there was a happy ending. Incredibly, Hurley returned to the Kings for the 1994–95 season. His shooting and his mobility weren't quite up to speed—he scored only 285 points in 68 games—but there were flashes of his past brilliance we will probably see in the future.

Bobby Hurley's 1995 statistics were nothing extraordinary, unless you consider that he was lucky to be alive, much less playing with some of the world's best athletes, like Karl Malone of the Utah Jazz.

Jammin'
Jimmy Jackson

When he missed the first 54 games of his professional career over a bitter contract dispute, people wondered about Jim Jackson's attitude. He had posted enormous numbers in three seasons at Ohio State, including a 22.4-point average as a junior, and the Dallas Mavericks made him the fourth choice of the 1992 draft. But for the longest time, he and the Mavericks couldn't come to terms.

Finally, Jackson signed a six-year deal on March 4, 1993. The next night, when Jackson scored just 6 points in his National Basketball Association debut, the critics probably smiled. One night later, however, Jackson smoked the Phoenix Suns with 19 points.

The Mavericks, who had lost 50 of 54 games without Jackson, won 7 of their remaining 28 games. Jackson, who finished the 1992–93 season with 7 straight 20-point games or better, posted a 16.3-point scoring average.

In 1993–94, Jackson took his place alongside some of the game's great guards. He averaged 19.2 points, 4.7 rebounds, and 4.6 assists per game. Jackson also showed toughness by playing in all 82 games, something only sixteen other players managed. His 388 rebounds were a team record for a guard. There was more: Jackson set another Mavericks standard with 3,066 minutes played, breaking Derek Harper's mark of 3,032 set in 1987–88.

Before the 1994–95 season began, Dallas Head Coach Dick Motta was asked what he thought of his six-foot-six-inch (198 cm), 220-pound (100 kg) guard. "There are some great shooting guards in the league," Motta said, "but considering age, strength, height, and attitude, if we got a call from anyone in the league on a two-guard to trade for Jim, I don't think I'd take anyone else. That's a pretty strong statement."

Motta knew that Jackson's uncommon size and strength allowed him to overpower most smaller guards on the offensive end. And defensively, he handled most of them just as easily and, on some occasions, was even asked to stop opposing forwards.

Jackson's only real fault was turnovers; his 334 led the league in 1993–94. But Motta had an answer for that: rookie Jason Kidd. With Kidd playing point guard, suddenly Jackson was free to do what he does best. And that means scoring points–in big bunches.

Jackson was among the league's scoring leaders in 1994–95, before an injury sidelined him. As it was, he averaged 25.7 points in 51 games, a figure that would have placed him at fifth overall. The way he is going, James Arthur Jackson will stand tall among guards—and all NBA players—for years to come.

A protracted holdout tainted his rookie season, but when Jimmy Jackson started to produce for Dallas, the Mavericks became bullish on the rest of the league.

> "There are some great shooting guards in the league, but...I don't think I'd take anyone else."
> —Dick Motta

The Slam Dunk

Back in those funky American Basketball Association days in the early 1970s, Julius Winfield Erving II created a new art. He was only a six-foot-seven-inch (200 cm) forward, but he somehow mastered the art of floating down the lane—the craft of defying gravity. And when Dr. J was operating, when he arrived at the basket, he unleashed a spectacle of muscle and grace. It was called a slam dunk and it brought people out of their seats. It became Erving's signature, and twenty years later it would become the status symbol of the National Basketball Association.

"The Doc changed ball," says Magic Johnson. "The Doc went past jumps, hooks, sets—went past everything—and made the playground official."

He grew up in Roosevelt, New York, and honed his game on the playgrounds in Harlem. When people started calling him "Black Moses" and "Houdini," he politely told them they could call him "Doctor."

Kevin Loughery, who was Erving's coach when he played for the New Jersey Nets from 1973–76, believes Dr. J is the most important figure in the game's history. "I honestly believe that Doc did more for pro basketball than anybody, on and off the court. Doc was the first guy to fly. He did things with a basketball that nobody else had ever done."

In today's game, slam dunks are a regular fact of life. And while there is an aggressive edge that was absent from Dr. J's slams, the basic shot itself is sound strategy. There is no higher percentage shot than the slam dunk; not only is it spectacular, it is efficient. That is why the players with the best field goal percentage are invariably large with a penchant for slamming. Orlando's Shaquille O'Neal, Seattle's Shawn Kemp, and Denver's Dikembe Mutombo are traditionally among the league's most consistent shooters.

Despite appearances, slam dunks are a skill that is learned. Think how many missed slams you see in a typical game. Judging your speed and the basket location in the traffic of a professional game can be difficult.

"Although the shot is spectacular and appears unrehearsed, it actually isn't," says Boston forward Dominique Wilkins, whose nickname—"The Human Highlight Film"—is based on his slams. "Your practices and scrimmages are the time to be creative with different dunks. This way you will have a good idea of what you can and cannot do in an actual game situation."

Above: This is Julius Erving at the top of his game. Dr. J turned heads at the American Basketball Association slam dunk competition by taking off at the foul line, some fifteen feet (4.5m) from the basket, and floating in for a resounding jam. Opposite, top: Boston Celtic Dee Brown put a new spin on an old trick by covering his eyes on the way to winning the NBA's 1992 slam dunk title. Opposite, bottom: Latrell Sprewell has the stuff of champions.

There was a time when the dunk was illegal. The National Collegiate Athletic Association actually banned the use of the shot in 1967 after Lew Alcindor (later known as Kareem Abdul-Jabbar) of UCLA tore up the college game with his devastating slams. A decade later, the NCAA realized that the slam dunk was a thing of beauty and returned the move to its proper place in the game.

And just when you think you've seen every slam dunk in the catalog, up pops a Terry Ross. A member of the Tri-City Chinook, Ross found himself in the 1995 Continental Basketball Association slam dunk finals. Needing a perfect dunk to defeat Pittsburgh's Kris Bruton, who had already executed three soaring jams, Ross stood on the baseline behind the basket. He threw the ball high over the backboard, took three steps forward, caught the ball in midair and completed a two-handed backward slam. Wow.

Grandmama
Larry Johnson

Growing up in Texas, Larry Demetric Johnson dreamed of knockouts and uppercuts. For five years, from 1978 to 1982, he toiled at the sweet science in the Police Athletic Boxing League. He was actually pretty good at it, but suddenly something ended his boxing career—height. When he looked in the mirror at age thirteen in seventh grade, Johnson already stood six foot two inches (187cm). Clearly, bigger things were in store.

As a senior at Skyline High School in Dallas, the man they call LJ was chosen as the United States High School Basketball Player of the Year. Not surprisingly, his classmates voted him Most Likely to Succeed—as a basketball player, not a boxer.

After two years at Odessa Junior College in Texas, Johnson powered the University of Nevada at Las Vegas to the 1990 national championship in his junior season. He averaged 20.6 points per game, improved that average to 22.7 as a senior, and was the obvious choice for the Wooden and Naismith Awards as the nation's best college player.

The Charlotte Hornets, picking first in the 1991 draft, did the right thing. They made Johnson, the man with the gold-toothed grin, the first choice, and the forward went on to have a textbook rookie season. He averaged 19.2 points and 11 rebounds, and walked away with the Rookie of the Year Award.

And then, somehow, Johnson got better. In his second NBA season, he averaged 22.1 points and 10.5 rebounds per game, finishing twelfth and thirteenth in the league in those categories. His 1,810 points were a team record. How polished was Johnson at this stage of his career? Well, there was only one other NBA player who averaged at least 20 points, 10 rebounds, and 4 assists, and that was Charles Barkley of the Phoenix Suns.

Looking for more proof? Johnson was the first Hornet in history to be named to the All-Star Game, and he started in the 1993 classic in Salt

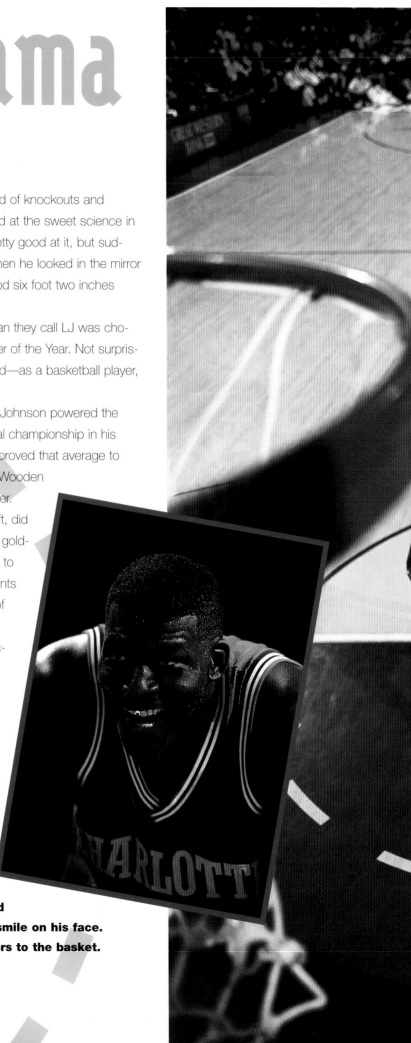

Inset: With his back problems apparently behind him, Johnson is approaching the future with a smile on his face.
Right: Johnson beats three Golden State Warriors to the basket.

Lake City. Johnson joined Shaquille O'Neal, Michael Jordan, and David Robinson as the only first- or second-year players in the previous decade to start an All-Star Game. He made something of a splash with sneaker commercials that depicted him as "Grandmama."

For two magnificent seasons, Johnson was very nearly perfect and the Hornets rewarded him with a twelve-year, $84 million contract. He played in all 164 of the Hornets' games, but late in the 1993–94 season a series of back injuries, including two herniated disks, knocked Johnson out of the lineup for the first time as a professional. Rest assured that Charlotte missed him. In the 31 games he was forced to sit out, the Hornets were just 9–22. When Johnson returned, his scoring and rebounding averages suffered, and he lacked his typical explosiveness.

In 1994–95, Johnson proved he was back, so to speak. He averaged 18.8 points per game, and both he and the Hornets appear to have a healthy future.

Whiz Kidd

Jason Kidd

Okay, so here is all you need to know about Jason Kidd: first of all, his middle name is Frederick. And then there is his pet rottweiler, Mia. Shoe size: 13½. Nicknames: the Whiz Kidd and the Jewel. Favorite actress: Julia Roberts. Favorite sport to watch (other than basketball): baseball. Favorite sport to play (other than basketball): golf. Oh, and his favorite kind of food is Chinese.

There are also a few basketball notes to pass on: in a way, it's unfair, for Jason Kidd's time has always been before him. By the time you read this, his moment in the big time may have actually arrived.

He was a high school player of astonishing ability in California. No one in state history ever recorded more than the 1,155 assists he posted for St. Joseph of Notre Dame. At the same time, Kidd led his team to a combined record of 63–6 during his last two seasons and two state Division I titles. Kidd was the country's best player as a senior, averaging 25 points, 10 assists, 7 rebounds, and 7 steals.

Kidd elected to stay home and play for the University of California, where he squeezed a terrific career into two short seasons. Kidd was honored as a first-team All-America as a sophomore after leading the nation with 227 assists, good for a new Pacific 10 and school record. Most impressive was Kidd's ability to raise the level of his game when the stakes were at their highest. In early 1994, Kidd helped upset top-ranked UCLA with one of his 4 career triple-doubles: 18 points, a career-high 14 rebounds, and 12 assists. He was also lethal on defense.

When the Dallas Mavericks stepped up in the 1994 draft, Glenn "Big Dog" Robinson was already gone. The next choice, naturally, was Kidd. Even before he appeared in his first NBA game, Kidd had a brush with greatness. He played on Michael Jordan's team in the Scottie Pippen charity All-Star Game, the last game ever played in Chicago Stadium. One of the game's best plays was a behind-the-back, off-the-backboard alley-oop pass to Anfernee Hardaway of the Orlando Magic.

Point guards are undersized by NBA standards, but they have nerves of steel. Even for a point guard, though, Jason Kidd has tremendous mettle, whether he's beating Spud Webb and the Sacramento Kings with a three-point shot (right) or penetrating inside against Chris Mullin and Latrell Sprewell of the Golden State Warriors (inset).

> **"Players love to play with him because you run the court, but if you get open you better be ready to catch it."**
> **—Dick Motta**

"He's a Bob Cousy–type passer, with quick, clever, look-away passes," said Dallas Head Coach Dick Motta. "Players love to play with him because you run the court, but if you get open you better be ready to catch it."

Kidd's presence at point guard in 1994–95 led to dramatic improvements for the Mavericks and their two other young stars, Jim Jackson and Jamal Mashburn. Kidd and Detroit's Grant Hill were the NBA's Co-Rookies of the Year. Kidd averaged 11.7 points, 7.7 assists, and 1.91 steals per game, and in April he had three triple-doubles in a three-week span.

That said, Kidd is still a future prospect. One national magazine recently voted him to the Dream Team 2000, along with Glenn Robinson, Shawn Kemp, Shaquille O'Neal, and Latrell Sprewell.

Laettner
Christian Laettner

Like a number of today's hoop heroes, Christian Laettner had a fairy-tale ride all the way to the National Basketball Association before hitting a rough patch of road. Because of the league's drafting system, the good teams draft last and the not-so-good teams draft first. This is why the Jim Jacksons and Chris Webbers and Christian Laettners wind up struggling on young teams during their first few years in the league.

Of course, young teams tend to improve with time. Look at the Orlando Magic team that managed to come up with Shaquille O'Neal and Anfernee Hardaway in back-to-back seasons. It is the hope for this kind of success that drives Laettner through his early seasons with the Minnesota Timberwolves. Certainly, his résumé suggests that success will come. It always has.

Opposite, top: Duke University's Christian Laettner was the only college player selected to the Dream Team for the 1992 Olympics in Barcelona, Spain. Now, he works for the Minnesota Timberwolves. Opposite, bottom: Laettner is not above throwing his considerable weight (245 pounds [111kg]) around under the basket.

Michael Williams

In the game of basketball there is one level playing field, a place where all men—from five-foot-three-inch (1.6 m) guards to seven-foot-six-inch (2.2 m) centers—are equals: the free throw line. Fifteen feet from the basket, take your best shot. Eight-year-olds can make them, but sometimes—like those short putts in golf for a lot of money—free throws can be very difficult under pressure. Concentration is the key.

Heading into the 1992–93 season, the man at the head of the class in concentration was Calvin Murphy, who played guard for the Houston Rockets from 1971 through 1983. Murphy finished his career with an .892 free-throw percentage, third all time behind Mark Price (.906) and Rick Barry (.900). In 1981, Murphy successfully made .958 of his free throws—the National Basketball Association single-season record. And, between December 27, 1980, and Feb. 28, 1981, Murphy did not miss once. He sank 78 straight free throws.

That standard stood for more than a decade. Michael Williams, a six-foot-two-inch (1.8 m), 175-pound (78.7 kg) guard, took that piece of history and made it his own. He had bounced around since 1988, playing with Detroit, Phoenix, Dallas, and Charlotte, as well as the Rapid City Thrillers of the Continental Basketball Association. After a stint in Indianapolis, Williams joined the Minnesota Timberwolves. On April 25, 1993, Williams, a study in focus and concentration, broke Murphy's record and ran his free throw streak without a miss to 84.

For Michael Williams the free throw line is indeed the charity stripe; in 1993 he hit a staggering 84 straight free throws.

Even in high school, at the Nichols School in Buffalo, New York, Laettner's teams were champions. Led by Laettner, Nichols won two New York State championships.

Laettner's four years at Duke may have been one of college basketball's most fulfilling careers. For starters, the six-foot-eleven-inch (210cm), 245-pound (111 kg) Laettner became the first player in college history to start in four National Collegiate Athletic Association Final Fours. The Blue Devils won the championship his last two seasons, 1991 and 1992. He averaged 19.8 points per game as a junior and 21.5 as a senior. He finished his career as only the third Duke player to record more than 2,000 points and 1,000 rebounds.

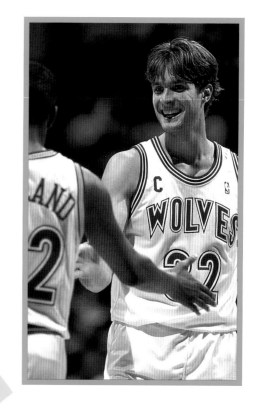

Perhaps the most memorable shot he ever took was an eighteen-foot (5.4m) turnaround jumper that beat Kentucky at the buzzer in the 1992 East regional finals. It was the tenth shot of the game for Laettner and his tenth basket, to go along with a perfect 10-for-10 from the free throw line.

Laettner became the NCAA's all-time leading scorer in tournament play with 407 points and won the Wooden and Naismith Awards as the nation's outstanding player. The Timberwolves made him the third overall choice of the 1992 draft, but before he joined the NBA, Laettner helped produce another golden memory.

Against long odds, he was selected as a member of the Olympic Dream Team. Laettner, in fact, was the only college player on a team that included Michael Jordan, Larry Bird, and Magic Johnson. And, though he played sparingly, Laettner received a gold medal.

Armed with a six-year, $21.6 million contract, Laettner went to work in Minnesota, but the results have not been so encouraging. The Timberwolves lost 186 games during Laettner's first three seasons, a disappointment only partly softened by his inclusion on the 1992 NBA All-Rookie team.

Named after Christian Diestl, a German soldier played by Marlon Brando in the 1958 film *The Young Lions,* Laettner now contemplates his future, along with the shark swimming in a three hundred-gallon (1,135.5l) tank in his home. Laettner hopes that the Timberwolves, like his favorite pet, show their teeth soon.

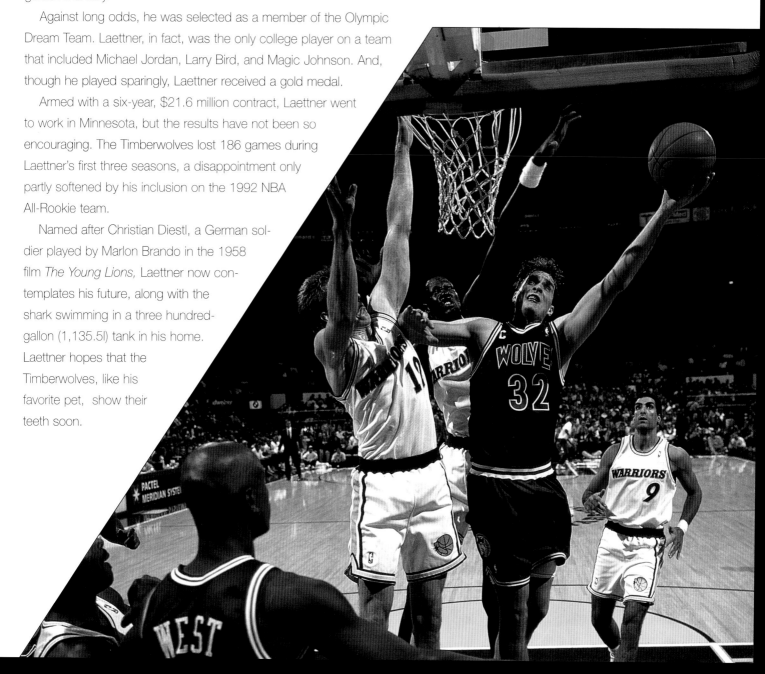

The Mash
Jamal Mashburn

The playground. This is where you find the basketball stars of the next generation. On the city asphalt, the only thing that determines who plays the games is ability. If your stuff isn't good enough for the playground, you'll find out in a hurry.

Growing up in New York City, Jamal Mashburn was a terrific playground player. He played at the Holcombe Rucker Memorial Playground, where legends like Connie Hawkins and Julius Erving learned the game. In 1990, Mashburn took Cardinal Hayes High School in the Bronx to its first New York City championship in forty-six years.

Later that same year, Mashburn decided to take his size 16 sneakers to Kentucky. It wasn't long before the six-foot-eight-inch (203cm), 240-pound (109 kg) forward began to make a similar impression. He played three seasons at Kentucky, averaging 21 points per game in his final two years. Mashburn took Kentucky to the Final Four as a junior, leading the Wildcats to a 30–4 record.

In all, Mashburn started each of the 98 games Kentucky played while he was there. And, despite playing only three seasons instead of the customary four, his 1,843 points gave him the fourth-highest total in school history. Mashburn was a consensus All-American and viewed by some as the national player of the year.

The Dallas Mavericks made him the fourth overall choice in the 1993 draft, believing he would be a natural scoring complement to guard Jim Jackson. And that's exactly how it worked out. Mashburn posted the highest scoring average for a fourth pick since the draft began in 1957, pumping in 19.2 points per game. This, despite drawing two and sometimes three defenders around the basket. After Jackson ended a long holdout, he, too, averaged 19.2 points per game, and the two became a potent scoring tandem.

Lost in Mashburn's success was his relatively tender age. At twenty, he was the league's second-youngest player to start the 1993–94 season (behind Chris Webber). He set seven Mavericks rookie records, including starts (73), minutes (2,896), and three-pointers (85).

In only his second year, averaged more than 24 points per game, more than many established all-stars. Above: The talented Mashburn, seen here splitting the Clippers defense, is often double teamed. Opposite: Jamal won't let anything stand in his way of winning. Here, he drives hard on the Lakers.ble teamed.

Mashburn's ability to shoot the three-pointer with finesse and still collect muscular rebounds makes him difficult to defend. In fact, early in the 1994–95 season the NBA got a taste of Mashburn's potential. One night Mashburn torched the Chicago Bulls for 50 points. Many of them came against Scottie Pippen, one of the league's best defenders.

The combination of Mashburn and Jackson has proved to be nearly unstoppable. Freed by opposing defenses forced to deal with Jackson and rookie point guard Jason Kidd, Mashburn's scoring average climbed to over 24 points per game by season's end—ahead of such stars as Patrick Ewing, Charles Barkley, and Clyde Drexler.

Mashburn's legend continues to grow. He already has all-world statistics, not to mention "The Mash" line of sneakers sponsored by Fila. The playground seems very far away. Or does it? One of his favorite hobbies is playing video games, such as John Madden Football, PGA Golf II, and Ms. Pac-Man.

Miller Time
Reggie Miller

Reggie Miller was just minding his own business, averaging 20 points a game for the Indiana Pacers, when destiny called. Maybe the line had been busy for seven seasons, but in the 1994 National Basketball Association playoffs, it was suddenly Miller Time.

In Game Five against the New York Knicks at Madison Square Garden, Miller put together one of the great quarters in the history of playoff basketball. He scored 25 of his career-high 39 points in the fourth quarter, an unconceivable stretch that included 5 three-point baskets, 3 field goals, and 4 free throws. The Pacers won the game, 93–86, to take a 3–2 series lead, but the Knicks eventually won in 7 games to take the Eastern Conference title.

And though Indiana watched as the Knicks challenged the Rockets for the NBA championship, Miller had emerged as one of the league's last pure jump shooters. In a league of aircraft carriers, Miller's slight six-foot-seven-inch (200cm), 185-pound (84kg) frame offers him few other options.

"Shooting is concentration and rhythm, and sometimes it is pure confidence," Miller said. "But you have to work at it. The common denominator among shooters is that we all worked hard to develop our shot. I don't think kids do that today. These days you don't go to the playground to shoot your J. You go to try to dunk on someone's head. I did that, too, but I always brought my jump shot with me."

Certainly he had a few genes working in his favor. Miller's sister Cheryl was a member of the 1984 United States Olympic basketball team that won a gold medal. His brother, Darrell, was a former major league catcher. Another sister, Tammy, earned a volleyball scholarship at California State-Fullerton.

> **"Shooting is concentration and rhythm, and sometimes it is pure confidence."**
> **—Reggie Miller**

Miller, here against Portland, has the speed to finish fast break layups (right), the touch to hit nothing but net from the three-point line (opposite, left), and the ball-handling skills to free himself of opponents who overplay his shot (opposite, inset).

John Stockton

This anonymous six-foot-one-inch (185cm), 175-pound (79kg) point guard came from a place called Gonzaga University in Spokane, Washington, and all he did was pass his way into the National Basketball Association record book.

John Stockton, the sixteenth overall selection in the 1984 draft, always had a keen court sense, a peripheral vision that allowed him to find teammates who didn't seem to be open. After three seasons of fairly modest results, Stockton made his mark in 1987–88. He broke the NBA's season assist mark set by Isiah Thomas (1,123), by recording 1,128 assists. Stockton would surpass Thomas' mark three more times and clear 1,000 assists six times in a seven-year span.

During the 1994–95 season, Stockton officially became the league's all-time leader. Heading in, he had trailed Magic Johnson (9,921 assists) and Oscar Robertson (9,887), but with the help of Utah forward Karl Malone and his Jazz teammates, Stockton passed those two legends and now has a total of 10,394. Stockton, who turned thirty-three late in the season, seems destined to run the record out of reach for the forseeable future.

No NBA player ever made more passes that set up baskets than John Stockton of the Utah Jazz. Here, he tees up another team-mate in the 1995 playoffs.

So, growing up in Riverside, California, there were always a lot of balls in the air. Lewis practiced his shot in his backyard, to the point where UCLA offered him a full scholarship. He left as the third-leading scorer in school history (2,095 points), which was quite an accomplishment considering the quality of its players over the years. Miller's shooting percentage at UCLA was .547, a terrific number for a guard who plays away from the basket.

The Pacers drafted him in the first round, eleventh overall, and his scoring average went from 10 points a game as a rookie to 16 points his second professional season to an amazing 24.6 his third season. That was the year he became the first Pacers all-star since 1977.

In 1992–93, Miller set a Pacers record and led the NBA with 167 three-pointers, 5 shy of the all-time record. In the summer of 1994, Miller was a tri-captain of Dream Team II, the United States team that participated in the world championships in Toronto. He averaged 17.1 points a game, second on the team of emerging all-stars. In 1994–95, Miller averaged 19.6 points per game and carried the Pacers past the Knicks in the playoffs.

Reggie Miller, seen here blowing past the New York Knicks' John Starks, is one of the game's most explosive players. Somehow he scored 25 points in the fourth quarter of a 1994 playoff game against the Knicks.

Zo
Alonzo Mourning

In any other year, in any other time, the man they call "Zo" would be the straw that stirs the drink, the main man. But unfortunately for Alonzo Mourning, he happened to come along at precisely the same time as Shaquille O'Neal. Regardless of what he achieves (and he's capable of plenty), Mourning will always be lost in the shadow of Shaq. That's okay, because there's a lot of room for success. And, for what it's worth, Mourning knows a little something about dealing with shadows.

For instance, he is one of forty-nine children raised by foster parent Fanny Threet in Chesapeake, Virginia. He played for Indian River High School there and caught the eye of Georgetown Coach John Thompson. It was Thompson who helped Patrick Ewing become a force in the college game, and Mourning was soon responding to his teaching, too—but not before the six-foot-ten-inch (208cm), 240-pounder (109 kg) was actually invited to the 1988 Olympic trials before ever stepping onto a college court.

Mourning became a wonderful defensive center, challenging every shot. In his freshman year, he led Division I with 169 blocked shots and an amazing average of 4.97. As a senior, Mourning again led all Division I players, including Shaq, with 160 blocks. All told, he blocked 453 shots, an NCAA record.

At the same time, Mourning developed offensive skills to go with his defense. In his last year at Georgetown he averaged 21.3 points per game, more than Ewing ever scored, plus 10.7 rebounds and 5 blocked shots. Mourning did something else Ewing never achieved: he was named the Big East Conference Player of the Year, the Defensive Player of the Year, and the Big East Tournament Most Valuable Player—all in the same season.

If O'Neal had attended Louisiana State University for a fourth season, Mourning would have been the first player taken in the 1992 draft. But as it was, the Orlando Magic selected Shaq first and the Charlotte Hornets drafted Mourning second overall.

That was almost exactly how they tore through the National Basketball Association as rookies. Mourning averaged 21 points

It was Alonzo Mourning's misfortune to follow Patrick Ewing at Georgetown University. However, when he didn't measure up physically as a rookie, Mourning built himself into a match for the league's best centers.

and 10.3 rebounds per game, second-best among rookies, while Shaq averaged 23.4 points and 13.8 rebounds. They were the only two unanimous choices for the All-Rookie team. To put their seasons in perspective, consider that the last rookie before them to average 20 points and 10 rebounds a game was center David Robinson in 1990.

Despite missing 21 games with a torn calf and a sprained ankle, Mourning improved his scoring average to 21.5 in his second year. He was also named to the All-Star team for the first time. Mourning is a powerful rebounding force, yet agile enough to run the floor like a small forward. When some of the league's centers wore him down as a rookie, he got stronger in the weight room. When you compare yourself with the best, there is always a little room for improvement.

Inset: The Charlotte Hornets' Alonzo Mourning can match-up with the likes of Patrick Ewing or just about anyone else. Bottom: Mourning is a solid force in the paint.

The Dream
Hakeem Olajuwon

You are Hakeem Olajuwon. You are seventeen years old. You are a terrific soccer player in your native land of Nigeria. Your name translates into "always being on top." Your best sport is actually handball. Then, at the All-Nigeria Teachers Sports Festival in Sokoto in 1978, fate intervenes. A basketball player named Akin Orinmoloye from your school, the Muslim Teacher's College, approaches your coach to see if they can borrow you for a few games. The answer is yes, and the rest is history.

Lesson: never be afraid to try new things, especially if you are headed for seven feet (213cm) tall and 255 pounds (115kg), and your feet require a size 17 shoe. His full given name growing up in Lagos, Nigeria, was Akeem Abdul Olajuwon. He changed his first name to Hakeem in 1991, but his real handle is still "The Dream."

Two years after he discovered basketball quite by accident, Olajuwon found himself playing for Coach Guy Lewis at the University of Houston. Considering the substantial learning curve, his progress was remarkable. By the time he was a senior, Olajuwon had become one of eight centers in history to lead his team to the NCAA's Final Four three straight times. He was the tournament's Most Outstanding Player in 1983 and a study in spectacular efficiency as a senior.

Olajuwon led all Division I players with a 13.5 rebounding average in 1984, not to mention 5.6 blocked shots. Although his offensive skills clearly needed polish (he averaged only 16.8 points per game), he was the national leader with a .675 field goal percentage. True, most of his shots were dunks from in close, but he faced two, sometimes three opponents on every trip toward the rim. What would Olajuwon accomplish as a pro, when he really began to grasp the game?

The answers were evident soon after the Houston Rockets made him the first pick of the 1984 draft. In a decade of NBA play, Olajuwon has never failed to average 20 points over the course of a season. On two occasions, 1988–89

In the 1995 NBA playoffs, Hakeem Olajuwon of the Houston Rockets became widely viewed as the league's best player. All he did was carry the Rockets, a team with little depth, to their second consecutive championship. Here, he drives against the Spurs' David Robinson in Game One of the Western Semi-Finals.

Moses Malone

Even in the National Basketball Association you will find them: those annoying hackers who have no sense of style. Big men, particularly, are often accused of this sort of foul behavior, but there have been some who defy the stereotype.

Take Wilt Chamberlain, the legendary seven-foot-one-inch (215cm) center, for instance. He was the most explosive scorer ever, but he had a velvet touch on defense. Chamberlain played in 1,045 career games and yet never, ever fouled out. In fact, he averaged fewer than 2 personal fouls per game over his fourteen seasons in the National Basketball Association.

On April 19, 1991, Atlanta center Moses Malone went Chamberlain one better: the six-foot-ten-inch (208cm) center broke his record by appearing in his 1,046th consecutive game without being disqualified with 6 personal fouls.

Malone had a glorious history in the seasons leading up to the record. The man who jumped to the NBA directly from Petersburg High School in Virginia was the league's Most Valuable Player in 1979, 1982, and 1983.

Malone, who was still playing at the age of forty in the 1994–95 season, also holds the NBA record for most free throws made and most offensive rebounds.

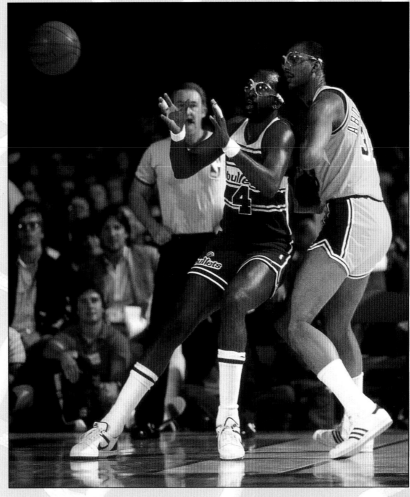

Malone was a master of the lean-in, though referees rarely called him for many offensive fouls.

Rick Barry Ends Wilt Chamberlain's Scoring Streak

In sports, team success often comes at the expense of individual accomplishment. Great players will invariably accept a less dominant role if it might lead toward the goal of a championship. So it was with Wilt Chamberlain in the 1966–67 season.

Chamberlain, a seven-foot-one-inch (215cm) center, entered the National Basketball Association in 1959 after a one-year stint with the Harlem Globetrotters and went on to lead the league in scoring. Then he did it again. In 1961–62, Chamberlain led with a 50.4-point average, while Chicago's Walt Bellamy was second with a 31.6 average. But Chamberlain's Philadelphia Warriors were eliminated in the Eastern Division semifinals by Syracuse.

Through the years, Chamberlain excelled, while the newly named 76ers continued to struggle. In 1965–66, he won his record seventh-straight scoring title with a 33.5-point average, but it was close for a change. Jerry West of the Los Angeles Lakers and Cincinnati's Oscar Robertson each averaged 31.3 points. The NBA's Rookie of the Year, Rick Barry, posted a tidy average of 25.7 for the Golden State Warriors.

In 1966–67, the 76ers looked like a championship team. Chamberlain took far fewer shots (1,150) than he had averaged over the previous seven seasons (2,438), and his scoring average fell to an earthly 24.1. Partly as a result of his unselfishness, the 76ers won the Eastern Division with a 68–13 record.

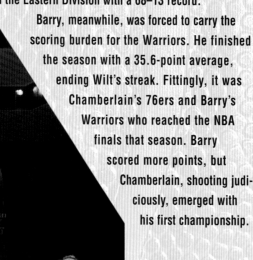

Barry, meanwhile, was forced to carry the scoring burden for the Warriors. He finished the season with a 35.6-point average, ending Wilt's streak. Fittingly, it was Chamberlain's 76ers and Barry's Warriors who reached the NBA finals that season. Barry scored more points, but Chamberlain, shooting judiciously, emerged with his first championship.

Rick Barry shoots a hook against the Cincinnati Royals.

and 1989–90, he led the league in points scored, the same years he led in total rebounds. Olajuwon is already third on the NBA's all-time blocked shot list, with 2,741. He also has the fourth-best scoring average among active players (23.7) and owns five Rockets records. In perhaps the most telling statistic, one that captures his breathtaking versatility, Olajuwon is the first and only player in the history of the league to record more than 200 blocks and 200 steals in the same season.

And then, at the age of thirty, Olajuwon produced his best season. He averaged a career-high 27.3 points, plus 11.9 rebounds, over the 1993–94 regular season. Olajuwon was magnificent in 23 playoff games, averaging 28.9 points and 11 rebounds per game. He made 46 points in the Portland series, 37 in Game Seven against Phoenix, and 25 points and 10 rebounds in Game Seven of the NBA finals. Olajuwon became the first player to win this trio of awards: the NBA Most Valuable Player, Defensive Player of the Year, and the NBA finals Most Valuable Player.

In 1994–95, Olajuwon became widely regarded as the game's best player. He didn't win the MVP Award, but his numbers (27.8 points and 10.8 rebounds) were better overall than the Spurs' David Robinson, who won the award. In the playoffs, Olajuwon outplayed Robinson and Shaquille O'Neal, leading the Rockets to their second consecutive NBA championship.

Hakeem Olajuwon, the Houston Rockets' peerless center, terrorized the NBA over the 1994–95 regular season and again in the playoffs. Here, he shoots over the Utah Jazz's Antonio Carr.

Hakeem Olajuwon   51

Shag Attack
Shaquille O'Neal

No one does it better these days in the National Basketball Association than Shaquille Rashaun O'Neal. At seven feet one inch (215cm), 303 pounds (137kg), and an unbelievable 8 percent body fat, he dominates the world of basketball, statistically, artistically, and commercially.

"Magic Johnson was a gifted orator," said Pat Williams, the general manager of the Orlando Magic. "Julius Erving was eloquent. Shaq? His greatest gift is his smile. He has got a facial expression for whatever he wants to say."

And on the court he's got the power and finesse to do whatever he wants as well. Some people wondered if the Magic made a mistake choosing O'Neal first overall in the 1992 draft with Alonzo Mourning available. But in three short seasons in the NBA, O'Neal went from a curiosity to the standard of excellence. Critics said he was too arrogant, too young, too busy off the court, but in addition to the movies, rap albums, and appearances, Shaq backed it all up with devastating numbers. At the 1995 All-Star break he was leading the league in scoring, pushing 30 points per game, and making more than $16 million a year, only a quarter of that for playing basketball—all at the age of twenty-two.

> **"He is the best center in the league. He has brought a new dimension to the game."**
> **—Hakeem Olajuwon**

A nationwide advertising poll of eleven- to seventeen-year-olds in 1994 named Shaq "the coolest person alive." He averaged 23.4 points per game as a rookie, sweeping first-year honors, but critics argued that the dunk was his only shot.

Over the summer he picked up a turnaround jumper and a passable hook shot. His second-year scoring average was a lofty 29.3, second in the league. His shooting percentage of .599 was first overall, backed by 13.2 rebounds (first) and 231 blocked shots (sixth).

No one has brought excitement to the game quite like Shaquille O'Neal of the Orlando Magic. He is shown here finishing another monster dunk.

Did you say versatility? In his first two NBA seasons, Shaq was the only league player ranked in the top ten in four NBA categories. Even when he was triple-teamed in the 1994 All-Star Game by David Robinson, Hakeem Olajuwon, and Shawn Kemp, Shaq managed to find the basket.

O'Neal led the NBA in scoring in 1994–95 with an average of 29.3 points and was third with a rebounding average of 11.4. O'Neal helped carry the young Magic into the league finals, where they lost to Houston.

But contrary to popular belief, Shaq does have a flaw—a big one. He can't shoot free throws. Through four NBA seasons, his foul shooting percentage hovered well below 60 percent.

Still, O'Neal seems to know his place in the game will come with time. "Hakeem is the best right now," O'Neal said. "If I was to be compared to any center, I'd like to be compared to him. He dresses nice. He can score inside, outside, free throws. Great player. I'll be there, one day. Soon as I get my free throws down, I'll be there."

Olajuwon himself disagrees. "I accept his compliment humbly," Olajuwon said. "But he is the best center in the league. He has brought a new dimension to the game. There has never been someone that big and that strong and that quick and that active. Shaq will win many championships, and he will win many MVPs."

Above: O'Neal performs off the court as well; here he raps in his 1995 home video. Left: While O'Neal's offense gets all the attention, his defense in the 1995 playoffs opened eyes all around the league.

Kareem Abdul-Jabbar Becomes the NBA's All-Time Scoring Leader

The two giants of the game briefly crossed paths, between 1969 and 1973. Wilt Chamberlain, the towering seven-foot-one-inch (215cm) center who played in Philadelphia, San Francisco, and Los Angeles, was the greatest offensive player the game had ever seen, but his career was coming to an end. Lew Alcindor, an incredibly agile and athletic seven-foot-two-inch (218cm) center, was making his mark for the Milwaukee Bucks.

As a rookie, Alcindor averaged 28.8 points per game and finished second to Chamberlain's teammate, Jerry West, in scoring in 1969. In 1970–71, as Kareem Abdul-Jabbar, he led the National Basketball Association in scoring and won the Most Valuable Player Award for the regular season. In the playoffs, Abdul-Jabbar led the Bucks to the NBA title and took home postseason MVP honors.

Two years later, Chamberlain finished up with the Los Angeles Lakers and left a historic legacy: 31,419 points, an average of 30.1 in his 1,045 games.

Most people imagined his point total would never be threatened, but Abdul-Jabbar wasn't one of them. Slowly, through the 1970s and the early 1980s, he closed the gap on Chamberlain. Abdul-Jabbar was not the dominant center that Chamberlain was, in terms of both presence and explosive scoring potential, but he ran the floor with grace and shot with more consistency. Abdul-Jabbar's greatest weapon was the skyhook, a sweeping hook shot that was virtually unblockable.

On April 5, 1984, the Lakers' Abdul-Jabbar flipped a medium-range skyhook at the basket from the right baseline against the Utah Jazz in a game in Las Vegas. The shot was good and Abdul-Jabbar was the NBA's most prolific scorer. When he retired after the 1988–89 season, he had scored 38,387 points, a record that should stand for some time.

Here it is, the most lethal weapon in the history of the NBA: The Skyhook of Kareem Abdul-Jabbar. Imagine an athletic seven-foot-two-inch player (215cm) jumping in the air and shooting down at the basket!

Pippen
Scottie Pippen

There aren't a lot of guys from Hamburg, Arkansas, with three National Basketball Association championship rings. There's only one: Scottie Pippen, and that's a fast-food fact. In a brilliant career move, Pippen wound up with the Chicago Bulls in 1987 and hitched a ride to fame and stardom with the fabulous Michael Jordan. So Pippen got his rings as the Bulls dominated the league in the early 1990s. On the downside, something was lost in the translation. That something, of course, was Pippen.

A brilliant player in his own right, Pippen suffered by comparison to one of the greatest players who ever lived. When Jordan left the Bulls after the 1993 season to pursue baseball, the world discovered what the Bulls had long known: Scottie Pippen was a major league player, too. At six feet seven inches (200cm) and 210 pounds (95 kg), Pippen is a versatile swingman who can match up with the league's toughest guards and forwards. His exceptionally long arms may be his best asset.

That all of this would come to pass wasn't always obvious when he began playing for Central Arkansas back in 1983. In fact, Pippen's freshman year was something of a disaster. He scored 85 points for the entire season. By the time he was a senior, Pippen had polished the fine points of his game. He averaged 23.6 points per game to go along with 10 rebounds and 4 assists. Pippen also discovered a fondness for the three-point shot, sinking 23 of 40 for a percentage of .575.

The Seattle SuperSonics liked Pippen's skills enough to draft him fifth overall in 1987. The Bulls engineered a trade by sending the rights to center Olden Polynice, a second-round draft choice, and the option to switch first-round picks in 1989.

Playing in the wake of Jordan, Pippen's statistics were never blinding. His scoring average settled in around 17 points per game, but there was more to his game than just points. He was a tenacious rebounder at both ends of the floor and his passing ability was superb. After Jordan, Pippen was probably most responsible for the Bulls' three consecutive championships.

Playing in the shadow of Michael Jordan, Scottie Pippen won three NBA championship rings. By 1995, when he could be seen blasting past Dominique Wilkins of the Boston Celtics, Pippen was recognized as a star in his own right.

Wilkens Passes Auerbach

Excellence is the common denominator in Lenny Wilkens' rich and glorious basketball career. He was a Hall of Fame player, then made a successful transition to NBA coach. In 1992, Wilkens was an assistant to Head Coach Chuck Daly on the United States Olympic basketball Dream Team.

Then on January 6, 1995, Wilkens did something many people thought impossible: he surpassed Red Auerbach of the Boston Celtics as the league's all-time winningest coach. The Atlanta Hawks defeated the Washington Bullets, 112–90, and Wilkens obtained his 939th NBA coaching victory.

Auerbach won 938 game in twenty seasons and Wilkens finished the 1994–95 season, his twenty-second, with 968 victories. After the season, Wilkens was named head coach of the 1996 U.S. Olympic basketball team.

He was recognized for his efforts: Pippen was a regular on the NBA's All-Defensive teams, and in 1993 he made the All-NBA third team, marking him as one of the league's very special players. In 1992, Pippen was a member of the Dream Team that won the Olympic gold medal in Barcelona, Spain.

In his first season without Jordan, Pippen emerged as his own man. He averaged 22 points per game, totaling a career-high 1,587 points. He added 629 rebounds, for the best average (8.7) of his career. There were also 403 assists and 211 steals. Pippen was consistent, too, scoring in double figures in each of the 72 games he played.

The 1994 All-Star Game was Pippen's finest moment. He scored a game-high 29 points, making 9 of 15 shots, and added 11 rebounds. For his effort, Pippen was voted the game's Most Valuable Player, becoming only the second Bull (Jordan was the other) to win that distinguished honor. In 1994–95, Pippen averaged 21.4 points per game and led the league with 232 steals.

At a lean 210 pounds (95kg), Pippen seems spare but has the power to go through defenders, as the Knicks' Patrick Ewing discovered in the 1994 playoffs.

The Dream Team

College basketball stars have played for the United States Olympic basketball team for years. K.C. Jones and Bill Russell, two future Boston Celtics, won gold medals in 1956. Oscar Robertson and Jerry West led the Americans in Rome four years later. Bill Bradley, a future New York Knick and U.S. Senator, played in 1964; Isiah Thomas and Buck Williams played in 1980; Michael Jordan and Patrick Ewing helped bring home the gold from Los Angeles in 1984.

But when professionals were permitted to compete for the first time in the 1992 Olympics, all teams before—and probably after—paled by comparison, for never had such a group of athletes with such glittering résumés been gathered to play for the same team at the peak of their powers.

The dazzling United States roster in Barcelona, Spain, was a collection of the best and brightest from the National Basketball Association: Jordan and Ewing (again), Magic Johnson, Larry Bird, Charles Barkley, Clyde Drexler, John Stockton, Karl Malone, David Robinson, Scottie Pippen, Chris Mullin, and collegian Christian Laettner.

They called it the Dream Team. There was criticism from some quarters that the United States, stung by upsets in recent years, was not exactly operating in the spirit of the Olympics. However, the global response to the NBA game was, well, ecstatic.

The Dream Team destroyed the competition. In fact, the biggest problems in the team's first 13 games was overconfidence. How is an athlete supposed to react when opponents like members of the Brazilian National Team ask for autographs and photographs together?

The finals in Barcelona were understandably anticlimactic. It was a rematch of an earlier tournament game against Croatia, which featured current NBA player Drazen Petrovic and future NBA player Toni Kukoc. Ten minutes into the game, Croatia actually led the Dream Team, but a 15–2 flurry sent the United States off to a 117–85 victory.

Petrovic (24 points) and Kukoc (16 points) didn't have much help. By contrast, the U.S. team had seven players in double figures: Jordan (22), Barkley (17), Ewing (15), Pippen (12), Johnson (11), Mullin (11), and Drexler (10).

"This," said Head Coach Chuck Daly, on loan from the Detroit Pistons, "was a majestic team. I understand 180 countries and three billion people watched this game. Somewhere, there's a twelve- or thirteen-year-old kid who dreams of being Magic or Michael or Larry or Patrick Ewing. That's good for the sport. It gives the people a dream, and they're trying to live out a dream."

Even Bird, who played only 12 minutes in what turned out to be the last game of his career, was moved. "The reason I played was because it was a good way for me to go out at this late point in my career. And one thing you can tell your kids is I played on the greatest team of all time."

The Dream Team, left to right: Christian Laettner, David Robinson, Patrick Ewing, Larry Bird, Scottie Pippen, Michael Jordan, Clyde Drexler, Karl Malone, John Stockton, Chris Mullin, Charles Barkley, and Magic Johnson.

The Admiral
David Robinson

When David Robinson was growing up, he had no idea he would one day stand seven feet one inch (215cm) and weigh 235 pounds (106kg). He liked basketball, but he wasn't sure the game was his future—until he began to grow in high school.

"When I was a kid, I did a lot of different things," Robinson said. "I tried so hard to find something I was really great at. Not just good, but really great. So when I grew to be six foot eight [203cm] in high school, and I started developing as a basketball player, I told myself, 'This is your thing. This is the thing to go after.'

"I don't like to lose at anything. I don't want to say it's pride in yourself, because I think that word is overused, but it's being able to feel good about yourself."

These days, Robinson feels very good about himself. He is one of the best play-ers in bas-

"I don't like to lose at anything."
—David Robinson

The Longest Game

Unlike baseball, where time is measured in balls and strikes, outs and innings, a game of basketball is usually confined to a finite 48 minutes. Still, there is an occasional overtime game when, on a given night, two teams are evenly matched. Even rarer is double overtime. How about six overtimes—30 minutes of extra time? It actually happened once, back on January 6, 1951.

With 3,300 spectators on hand at the Edgerton Sports Arena in Rochester, the hometown Royals took on the Indianapolis Olympians. Rochester was working on a 7-game winning streak, but the score at the end of regulation was even at 65. Both teams were deliberate in their offenses, and two of the overtimes would be scoreless periods because one team chose to hold the ball for a single potential game-winning launch.

In the fifth overtime, Arnie Risen scored both of the Royals' baskets to force the sixth extra session. With the score tied at 73, Rochester took control of the ball early in the 5-minute period, intending to hold for the final shot. But the Olympians played aggressive defense and forced two ill-advised shots by Rochester. Alex Groza of Indianapolis grabbed a rebound and forced an outlet pass to teammate Ralph Beard, who hit a twelve-foot shot (3.6m) with 1 second left on the clock. It was the winner.

Three years later, the NBA sped up the game by introducing the 24-second clock, making it mandatory for teams to shoot the ball on each possession before the clock ticked down. And while the games became more offensive in nature and more exciting overall, it is likely there will never be another game like the one played by the Olympians and Royals.

David Robinson, here jamming on the Houston Rockets, will be a muscular force in the middle for years to come.

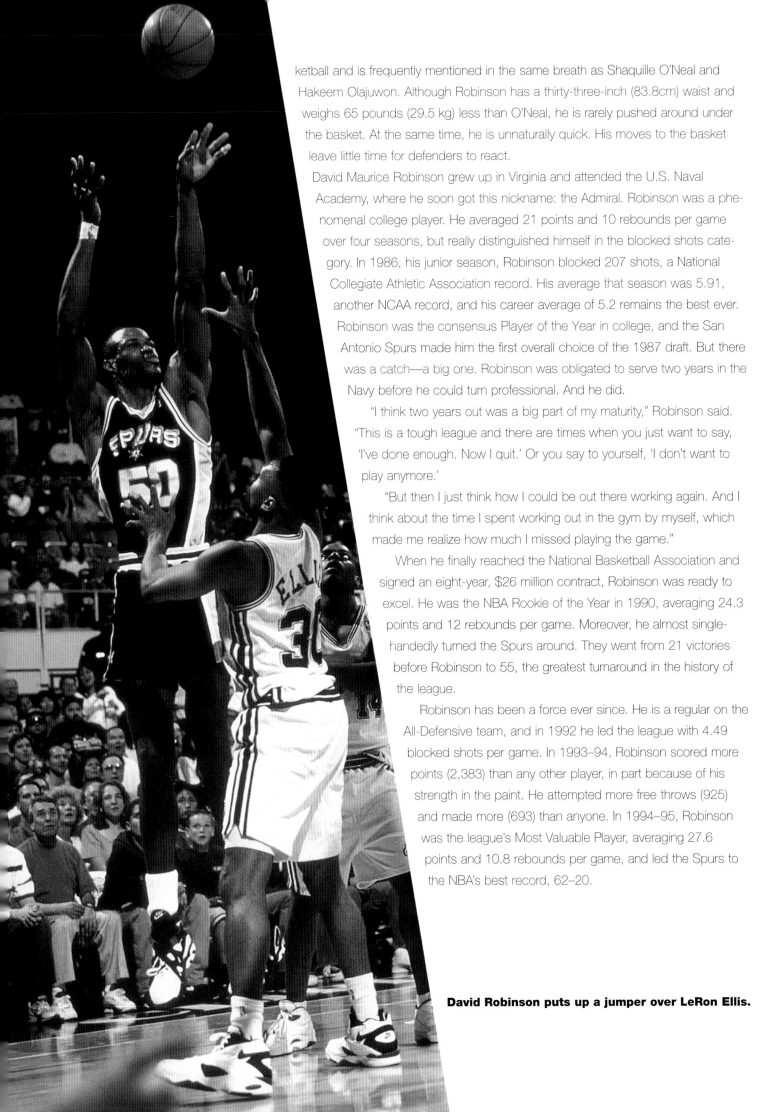

ketball and is frequently mentioned in the same breath as Shaquille O'Neal and Hakeem Olajuwon. Although Robinson has a thirty-three-inch (83.8cm) waist and weighs 65 pounds (29.5 kg) less than O'Neal, he is rarely pushed around under the basket. At the same time, he is unnaturally quick. His moves to the basket leave little time for defenders to react.

David Maurice Robinson grew up in Virginia and attended the U.S. Naval Academy, where he soon got this nickname: the Admiral. Robinson was a phenomenal college player. He averaged 21 points and 10 rebounds per game over four seasons, but really distinguished himself in the blocked shots category. In 1986, his junior season, Robinson blocked 207 shots, a National Collegiate Athletic Association record. His average that season was 5.91, another NCAA record, and his career average of 5.2 remains the best ever. Robinson was the consensus Player of the Year in college, and the San Antonio Spurs made him the first overall choice of the 1987 draft. But there was a catch—a big one. Robinson was obligated to serve two years in the Navy before he could turn professional. And he did.

"I think two years out was a big part of my maturity," Robinson said. "This is a tough league and there are times when you just want to say, 'I've done enough. Now I quit.' Or you say to yourself, 'I don't want to play anymore.'

"But then I just think how I could be out there working again. And I think about the time I spent working out in the gym by myself, which made me realize how much I missed playing the game."

When he finally reached the National Basketball Association and signed an eight-year, $26 million contract, Robinson was ready to excel. He was the NBA Rookie of the Year in 1990, averaging 24.3 points and 12 rebounds per game. Moreover, he almost single-handedly turned the Spurs around. They went from 21 victories before Robinson to 55, the greatest turnaround in the history of the league.

Robinson has been a force ever since. He is a regular on the All-Defensive team, and in 1992 he led the league with 4.49 blocked shots per game. In 1993–94, Robinson scored more points (2,383) than any other player, in part because of his strength in the paint. He attempted more free throws (925) and made more (693) than anyone. In 1994–95, Robinson was the league's Most Valuable Player, averaging 27.6 points and 10.8 rebounds per game, and led the Spurs to the NBA's best record, 62–20.

David Robinson puts up a jumper over LeRon Ellis.

The All-Star Game

As the National Basketball Association has enjoyed increased popularity in recent years, the All-Star Game has become an important event in sports, rivaling baseball's mid-summer classic. These days, the game is the centerpiece of a weekend of festivities, from the Legends Game to the All-Rookie Game to the slam dunk and three-point contests.

Boston's Larry Bird won the first three-point contest in 1986, helping it gain national attention. In 1991, defending champion Craig Hodges of Chicago joined Bird as the only two-time winner. In the semifinals against Portland's Terry Porter, Hodges hit his first 19 three-point shots, breaking Bird's record of 11 consecutive shots.

In 1991 Dee Brown, the Celtics' six-foot-one-inch (185cm) guard, won the slam dunk contest, defeating favorite Shawn Kemp, a six-foot-ten-inch (208cm) forward. The dunk that brought the crowd to its feet was completely original. Brown took off for the basket, closed his eyes and covered them with his free arm, and somehow found the hoop for a terrific slam.

Some of the best players in history have appeared in the NBA All-Star Game. Who played in more games than any other player? Kareem Abdul-Jabbar, the leading scorer of all time, played in 18. Next in line are Wilt Chamberlain, Bob Cousy, and John Havlicek, with 13 each. Not surprisingly, Abdul-Jabbar is the game's leading scorer, with 251 points, followed by

For several years Mitch Hammond has been one of the NBA's best anonymous players. In the 1995 All-Star Game the Sacramento Kings guard made a name for himself by scoring 23 points in 22 minutes.

Oscar Robertson (246), Bob Pettit (224), and Julius Erving (221). The all-time assists leader? Magic Johnson, of course, with 115. All-time steals? Isiah Thomas, with 26. Blocks? Abdul-Jabbar, with 31.

The game itself has become a study in offense. Or is that a lack of defense? The 1995 game in Phoenix was a typical contest, with the West beating the East, 139–112. Guard Mitch Richmond, who plays in obscurity for the Sacramento Kings, laid claim to being the game's premier perimeter shooter. He hit 10 of 13 shots and scored 23 points in a scant 22 minutes. Richmond was the runaway choice for Most Valuable Player. He became the first nonstarter to win the award since Tiny Archibald of the Celtics in 1981. His West teammates saw it coming midway through the fourth quarter.

"They told me to go in there and wrap it up," said Richmond, who scored 10 points in the fourth quarter. Shaquille O'Neal, who was triple-teamed by West defenders in his first All-Star appearance, broke through with a big game. He scored 22 points and added 7 rebounds.

The Detroit Pistons' Grant Hill, the first rookie to lead all vote-getters in All-Star history, did not get special treatment from the veterans. Hill finished with 10 points, but the game took its toll. "I kept asking Joe Dumars, 'Why am I so tired?'" Hill said. "It was from nerves. I was sick to my stomach in the second half and had to hurry up and get back to the bathroom."

Big Dog
Glenn Robinson

Fact: since 1971, only seven college underclassmen have declared themselves eligible for the National Basketball Association draft and been taken with the top pick: Magic Johnson, Los Angeles Lakers; Mark Aguirre, Dallas Mavericks; James Worthy, Los Angeles Lakers; Hakeem Olajuwon, Houston Rockets; Shaquille O'Neal, Orlando Magic; Chris Webber, Orlando Magic; and Glenn Robinson, Milwaukee Bucks.

This is pretty much all you need to know about Big Dog Robinson, the finest college player in the nation in 1994. Yes, the six-foot-seven-inch (200cm), 240-pound (109 kg) forward is that good.

He grew up in basketball-crazy Indiana, leading Roosevelt High School in Gary to a 30–1 record and a state championship. Robinson averaged better than 25 points, 14 rebounds, and 3 blocked shots, and actually tied

Like the truly great forwards in NBA history, Glenn Robinson has the speed to turn the corner on defenders, like Anthony Mason of the Knicks (above), and take the ball to go the hoop with authority (right).

with Webber as the National Player of the Year. Robinson stayed home for college, selecting tradition-rich Purdue University. He averaged 24 points and 9 rebounds per game as a sophomore, marking the first time a first-year player led the Big Ten in scoring since 1972. And then Robinson really broke through in his junior season. Part of his success is due to the power in his legs: Robinson's vertical leap is an extraordinary thirty-four inches (86.3cm). He was bigger, stronger, and quicker than most of the forwards he faced and his numbers proved it.

Robinson averaged 30.3 points per game, and his total of 1,030 points was the thirteenth-highest total ever for a single season. In Big Ten games, Robinson actually went himself one better, averaging 31.1 points. He was a force on the boards, too, averaging 9.7 rebounds. Robinson became the first player to lead the Big Ten in scoring and rebounding since Minnesota's Mychal Thompson in 1977–78.

The crowning achievement: Robinson won the Wooden Award as the country's best player. The award is named for John Wooden, the celebrated UCLA coach, who was, by the way, a standout at Purdue. In fact, Robinson was the first Boilermaker player so honored, going all the way back to Wooden's senior season in 1932.

The Milwaukee Bucks, who had been having hard times, selected Robinson with the first overall pick in the 1994 draft. He was only the third number one pick in team history, joining Kareem Abdul-Jabbar (1969) and Kent Benson (1977). Even before he wore a Milwaukee uniform, Robinson distinguished himself among professional players. On August 5, his team of all-stars played a charity game against a team captained by Magic Johnson. And though Johnson's team won, 166–155, Robinson scored more points than anyone—an even 50.

By the 1995 All-Star break, Robinson had already proved he belonged with the big dogs. And by the end of the season, Robinson was one of the league's legitimate stars. He finished with a scoring average of 21.9.

Glenn Robinson   65

The Worm
Dennis Rodman

It's easy to dismiss Dennis Rodman as a player who places style over substance. After all, "The Worm" appeared during the 1994–95 season for the San Antonio Spurs wearing, at various times, blue, blond, fuchsia, and purple hair. He has a variety of visually captivating tattoos. He wears a number of earrings. And yes, Rodman has been seen in the company of Madonna, that rock 'n' roll material girl.

On the other hand, Rodman is a terrific basketball player who is as unprecedented on the court as he is off it. Check this out: Rodman is a relatively slight six feet eight inches (203cm) and 210 pounds (95 kg), yet he led the National Basketball Association in rebounding for three consecutive seasons, from 1992 through 1994. Only three players in league history have more rebounding titles, and they are all legendary centers: Wilt Chamberlain (eleven), Moses Malone (six), and Bill Russell (five).

Listen to Chuck Daly, Rodman's coach for the Detroit Pistons when the team won back-to-back NBA championships in 1989 and 1990: "He's a unique player and maybe basketball will never see another one like him. He runs the floor, rebounds as well as anyone, plays great defense, has tremendous enthusiasm, and scores by happenstance. I never had a player like him."

More Rodman fun facts: Dennis Keith Rodman did not—repeat, did not—play high school basketball at South Oak Cliff in Dallas, Texas. He began his career in 1982 at Cooke County Junior College in Texas, producing almost as many rebounds (212) as points (281). For the next three years, Rodman played for Southeastern Oklahoma State, averaging more than 25 points and 13 rebounds per game. The Pistons chose him in the second round of the 1986 draft with the twenty-seventh overall selection.

Rodman fit in quickly as an unselfish, big-rebounding forward who scored points as an afterthought. On a team that included such scorers as guards Isiah Thomas and Joe Dumars and center Bill Laimbeer, this was just what Daly was looking for. Rodman's rebound total climbed every season as the Pistons rose to the top of the NBA.

When Detroit won the 1989 championship, Rodman was a league leader, but not in rebounding. He was actually first in shooting percentage (.595) because most of his shots followed offensive rebounds and came from in close. Rodman was

No one made a bigger splash during the 1995 season than Dennis Rodman of the San Antonio Spurs. Whether his hair was green, blond, or fuchsia, he was far and away the league's most relentless rebounder.

"He's a unique player and maybe basketball will never see another one like him."
—Chuck Daly

also voted to the NBA's All-Defensive first team for the first time. After Detroit won its second title in 1990, Rodman was honored as the league's Defensive Player of the Year.

Rodman repeated as Defensive Player of the Year in 1991 and produced 1,026 rebounds, 361 of them on the offensive end, to lead the league. In 1991–92, Rodman broke new ground by collecting an amazing total of 1,530 rebounds, an average of 18.7 a game. It was his first of four rebounding titles. Rodman's average in 1992–93 was 18.3, 17.3 the following season, and 16.8 in 1994–95. Rodman distinguished himself by becoming the first forward to win three consecutive rebounding titles.

The bird can't always catch The Worm: Dennis Rodman flies over two Atlanta Hawks for a rebound.

The Landlord
Latrell Sprewell

You can see most of today's National Basketball Association stars coming about 17 slam dunks away. Those players selected among the top five in each year's draft have the size, speed, and potential to be dominant. With refined scouting techniques and the proliferation of games on television, future stars don't slip through the cracks very often.

Still, once in a great while a Latrell Sprewell materializes, almost out of thin air. The six-foot-five-inch (195cm), 190-pound (86 kg) guard was the Golden State Warriors' first-round choice in the 1992 draft, but he was the twenty-fourth overall choice. And now, he is recognized as one of the game's great players. Everyone raves about Sprewell.

"Next to Michael Jordan, he's got to be the quickest two-guard [shooting guard] with the ball that I've ever played against," Reggie Miller of the Indiana Pacers said. "He can shoot, run the floor, jump, and he doesn't get tired."

Said Mitch Richmond of the Sacramento Kings: "Obviously, he has surprised a lot of people, because look where he was drafted. I didn't know who he was at first. Now everybody knows who he is. Some guys get better after they get in the league. He's one of them."

Latrell Fontaine Sprewell has always snuck up softly on people. He played in obscurity at Three Rivers Community College in Poplar Bluff, Missouri, from 1988 to 1990, averaging 21 points per game before moving to the University of Alabama for his last two college seasons. As a senior, Sprewell was one of four players named to both the All-Southeastern Conference first team and the All-SEC Defensive team. The others: future NBA first-round picks Alabama teammate Robert Horry, Lee Mayberry of Arkansas, and Shaquille O'Neal of Louisiana State University.

Sprewell showed potential as a rookie, averaging 15.4 points per game in the 1992–93 season. And although he was the first rookie in Golden State history to produce 1,000 points, 250 rebounds, 250 assists, 100 steals, and 50 blocked shots in a season, his versatility did not land him a spot on the league's All-Rookie first team.

He was not among the one hundred players listed on the 1994 All-Star ballot, but the coaches added him to the roster, making him the first player to achieve that feat since Detroit center Bill Laimbeer eleven years earlier. By the end of the 1993–94 season, Sprewell was a household name.

Sprewell showed his durability by playing in all 82 games and logging 3,533 minutes (an average of 43), more than any other NBA player and the highest league total since Len Robinson played 3,638 minutes for the New Orleans Jazz in 1977–78. Sprewell became an offensive threat, averaging 21 points per game, eleventh in the league. He also made a franchise record 141 three-point field goals. At the same time, Sprewell averaged 2.2 steals per game, ninth overall, and was honored as the youngest guard (twenty-three) ever named to the NBA All-Defensive team. In 1994–95, Sprewell averaged 20.6 points per game.

"Our coaches and I sit around and think about how good he's going to be," former Warriors coach Don Nelson said. "The sky is the absolute limit for Latrell Sprewell."

Inset: Latrell Sprewell, here driving on the Clippers, averaged 20.6 points per game over the 1994–95 season. Left: Sprewell shows why he is one of the NBA's rising stars as he twists and shoots.

"Next to Michael Jordan, he's got to be the quickest two-guard with the ball that I've ever played against."
—Reggie Miller

Webber

Chris Webber

The bottom line in basketball, as with any sport, is the final score—which is why points are the commodity prized above all others. But the great players master all the game's skills, even the subtle ones.

Consider, then, Chris Webber. In his rookie season of 1993–94, Golden State's six-foot-ten-inch (208cm), 250-pound (113 kg) forward did something no player ever did in his first National Basketball Association season: he totaled more than 1,000 points, 500 rebounds, 250 assists, 150 blocked shots, and 75 steals. In fact, only three players have ever strung together those kinds of numbers, and their names are Kareem Abdul-Jabbar, Hakeem Olajuwon, and David Robinson.

For the record, Webber produced 1,333 points (a 17.5 average), 694 rebounds (9.1), 272 assists (3.6), 164 blocks (2.2), and 93 steals (1.2). Thus, the league's youngest player—Webber was twenty-one—won the NBA Rookie of the Year Award. He led all rookies in rebounds, field goal percentage (.552), dunks (219), and blocks. Webber also became the youngest Warrior to lead the team in rebounding.

No wonder Webber is supremely confident. "I'll say this, I don't care who I'm playing against," Webber said. "I'm betting on myself."

Great things were always predicted for Mayce Edward Christopher Webber III. He was born in Detroit, where his father is a foreman at the General Motors Cadillac Division. Webber, who once scored 64 points and threw down 15 dunks in an eighth-grade game, led his high school team, Detroit Country Day, to three state titles. In 1990–91, he was the consensus National High School Player of the Year.

As one of Michigan's Fab Five Freshman in 1992, Webber helped the Wolverines become the surprise of the National Collegiate Athletic Conference Tournament. Seeded sixth in the Southeast Regional, Michigan won 5 straight games and advanced to the final opposite Duke before losing. In 1993, Michigan reached the NCAA championship game again, this time drawing North Carolina.

Webber made dubious history by calling time-out with 11 seconds left in the game when Michigan, trailing by 2 points at the time, was out of time-outs. As a

Above: When he was playing, Webber left mouths open in 1994–95. Opposite: While Chris Webber was dogged at Michigan for calling a time-out he didn't have and for his feud with Golden State Warriors Coach Don Nelson, no one questioned his ability on the basketball court. Here, he beats Charles Oakley of the New York Knicks to a rebound.

result, a technical foul was called on Michigan and North Carolina went on to win, 77–71. Still, Webber became the first player in history to make the NCAA All-Tournament team as a freshman and a sophomore. Webber also has the distinction of having his rights owned by three NBA teams in his first two seasons. He was drafted by the Orlando Magic first overall in 1993, then traded to Golden State for Anfernee Hardaway and three first-round picks. Then, after his marvelous rookie season, Webber was dealt again, this time to the Washington Bullets on November 17, 1994, for versatile power forward Tom Gugliotta, plus first-round picks for 1996, 1998, and the year 2000. Although he only played in 54 games in 1994–95, Webber averaged 20.1 points and 9.6 rebounds per game.

"I'll say this, I don't care who I'm playing against. I'm betting on myself."
—Chris Webber

THE
TEAMS

Bulls
Chicago

His high-ness, Air Jordan, arrived in Chicago as a rookie in 1984. And as magnificent as his individual gifts were, the team known as the Bulls left something to be desired. For six seasons, Michael Jordan labored, winning the National Basketball Association scoring title in the last four. Chicago, however, couldn't get past the Detroit Pistons, who won the Eastern Conference for three straight years, from 1988 through 1990.

Then, in the 1990–91 season, the Bulls finally broke through. Jordan had his usual spectacular year, leading the league in scoring for a fifth consecutive season with 31.5 points a game, but he also got some help from his teammates. Forwards Scottie Pippen (17.8 points per game) and Horace Grant (8.4 rebounds), center Bill Cartwright, and guard John Paxson rallied around Jordan. Together they carried the Bulls to new heights.

The Bulls' regular-season record was a snappy 61–21 and they rolled through the playoffs with ease. They swept the New York Knicks, then eliminated the Philadelphia 76ers in 5 games. Chicago torched the reigning champions, sending them back to Detroit with a stunning 4-game sweep. In the finals, even the Los Angeles Lakers provided little opposition. It was all over in 5 games and the image of Jordan, the Most Valuable Player in the finals, hugging the championship trophy even moved some fans of the Lakers and Pistons.

So, could the Bulls follow their first-ever title with a second? "Can we repeat? Well, yes," Jordan said. "Will we? There are a lot of variables involved, so I can't make any promises. I don't know if I'll ever have the same feeling as I did last June when we beat the Lakers. The emotions people saw in me and my teammates were ones of hard work.

"I do know this: now that I've tasted one championship, I definitely want another one." History suggested it was a difficult task. Beyond the Pistons, who won in 1989 and 1990, only the Celtics and Lakers had managed to win back-to-back championships. Well, it wasn't even close.

The Bulls won 67 games in the regular season, then put away the Knicks and the Cleveland Cavaliers before finding themselves in the 1992 finals against

The Bulls swarm underneath the basket against the Lakers in the 1991 Finals. In the 1990–91 season Jordan finally got the support he needed to bring a championship to Chicago.

Inset: Even the return of Michael Jordan in 1995 wasn't enough to recapture the Magic for the Chicago Bulls. Below: The Bulls jump in excitement as Game Six of the 1993 Finals ends and they become champions for the second year in a row.

the Portland Trail Blazers. The first game was Jordan's finest: he scored 35 points in the first half alone, including 6 three-point baskets. The Bulls won at Chicago Stadium. With the series tied at 2 games each, Jordan raised the level of his game again. He scored 46 points in Chicago's victory. Game Six also belonged to Jordan. He scored 33 points, 12 in the fourth quarter to rally the Bulls from a 15-point deficit and give them their second title.

Chicago made it 3 for 3 in 1993. The Bulls joined the Minneapolis Lakers (1952–54) and the Boston Celtics (1959–66) as the only teams to win three or more consecutive championships, this time dusting the Phoenix Suns in the final.

The Bulls' glorious run ended abruptly when Jordan retired to take up baseball. He left the game as the highest-scoring player in playoff history. Jordan's average per game of 34.7 is 5.6 points higher than the second-best figure, posted by Lakers guard Jerry West.

When Jordan returned in March 1995, the Bulls were in fourth place in the Eastern Conference's central division, and were a team looking for direction. Jordan's presence elevated Chicago above the mediocre teams, but the Bulls and their superb star fell to the Orlando Magic in the second round of the playoffs, thus failing to recapture the glory of the early 1990s.

Michael Jordan Returns

Michael Jordan left basketball in a blaze of glory, with three National Basketball Association championship rings and seven consecutive scoring titles. He walked away after the 1992–93 season precisely because he had done it all. They retired his number 23 jersey at Chicago Arena. Baseball, a sport he had never mastered, became his new passion.

He spent most of 1994 in Birmingham, Alabama, playing Double A baseball in the Chicago White Sox organization. He batted .202—hardly the stuff of champions—but he kept working on his game. In 1995, with the major league players on strike, Jordan walked away from his new game.

Twenty-one months after he left basketball, Jordan returned to the Chicago Bulls on March 19. The Bulls lost to the Indianapolis Pacers, 103–96, in overtime, but the double-pump fakes, the gravity-defying midair moves, and the explosive dribbles to the basket were all still there. His shooting, understandably, was not. Jordan, wearing number 45, missed 21 of 28 shots, but finished with 19 points, 6 assists, 6 rebounds, and 3 steals. He averaged 26.9 points in 17 regular-season games, but couldn't prevent the Bulls from losing to Orlando in the second round of the playoffs.

"The expectation is, 'Can he do the same things he did two years ago?'" Jordan said. "I look forward to the challenge. I tried to stay away as much as I could, but when you love something so long and you walk away from it, you can only stay away so long."

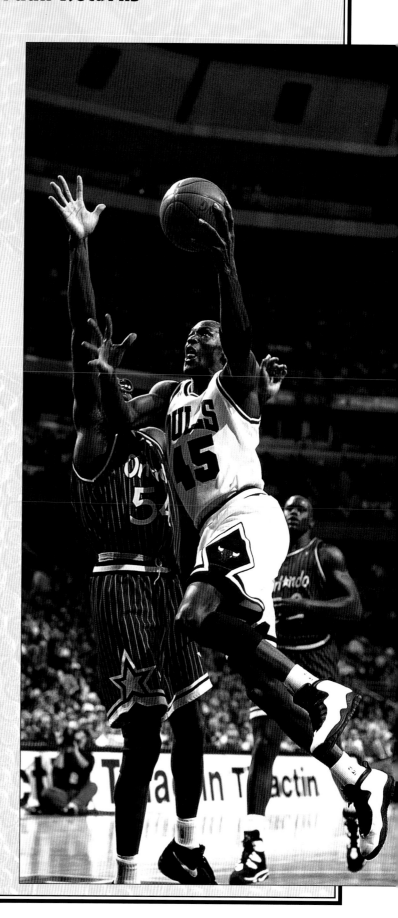

Upon returning to basketball Jordan wore number 45, but later reclaimed his old number 23 from the rafters. Here he drives against his old teammate, Horace Grant.

Celtics
Boston

In 1995, basketball lost a marvelous piece of history. That was the last season the Boston Celtics played at Boston Garden. Hanging high in the dusty rafters were sixteen National Basketball Association championship banners, monuments to excellence that may never be matched.

Through the years the Celtics have been basketball's most storied franchise; their feisty green leprechaun is an international symbol for basketball success. The list of names in the team record book reads like a Who's Who of the Basketball Hall of Fame: Red Auerbach, Bill Russell, K.C. Jones, Bob Cousy, Sam Jones, Tommy Heinsohn, John Havlicek, Larry Bird, Kevin McHale, and Robert Parish.

It all started with Auerbach, who built the Celtics' first championship with his own hands. As Boston's head coach and general manager, Auerbach made one of history's best trades, sending two of his best players, Ed Macauley and Cliff Hagan, to the St. Louis Hawks for the draft choice that would turn out to be a skinny six-foot-ten-inch (208cm) center named Bill Russell. Wonder of wonders, the Celtics defeated the Hawks in the seventh game of the 1956–57 championship series.

The Hawks beat the Celtics in the 1957–58 finals, and then Boston made history. Auerbach, with a truly breathtaking machine in place, presided over a team that won eight consecutive championships. No team in major professional sports history—the San Francisco 49ers, the New York Yankees, or the Montreal Canadians—ever approached that total.

The last jewel in the crown was the 1965–66 championship. The Celtics, trailing the Los Angeles Lakers, 2 games to 0, rallied to force a seventh game. Boston won, 95–93, and Auerbach took delight in lighting up his final victory cigar as coach. Auerbach passed the coaching responsibilities on to Russell, who responded by guiding the Celtics to back-to-back titles in 1967–68 and 1968–69. That gave Russell eleven championships in thirteen professional seasons, an unprecedented ratio of success.

Above: Head Coach Red Auerbach and forward Tommy Heinsohn celebrate a Celtics victory in 1957. Right: Larry Bird, the quintessential selfless Celtic, drives into Junior Bridgeman of the Milwaukee Bucks.

With John Havlicek and a different cast of characters—Jo Jo White, Dave Cowens, Don Chaney, and Don Nelson—the Celtics won titles in 1973–74 and 1975–76. The coach? Auerbach, who liked to keep the reins in the Celtics family, had given the job to Heinsohn.

In 1976, Auerbach pulled off another coup. In 1978, he drafted Larry Bird as a junior-eligible. While Bird carried Indiana State University to the National Collegiate Athletic Association championship game that year, the Celtics finished last in the NBA's Atlantic Division with a 29–53 record. One year later, with Bird averaging 21.3 points and 10.4 rebounds per game, the Celtics won their division with a 61–21 record.

Since joining the league in 1979–80, Bird and Magic Johnson of the Los Angeles Lakers dominated. For the next nine years, one or both of them found themselves in the championship series. Bird would prevail three times, leading the Celtics to three more titles: 1980–81, 1983–84, and 1985–86.

Robert Parish

He was born on August 30, 1953, in Shreveport, Louisiana, and during the 1994–95 season he was, at forty-one years of age, old enough to be the father of some of his young Charlotte Hornets teammates. And yet, Robert Parish, the seven-foot (2.1 m) center, played on.

He had four productive seasons for the Golden State Warriors, before the Boston Celtics' general manager, Red Auerbach, put together a sly 1980 trade that helped bring "The Chief" three championship rings. Parish, supported by fellow future Hall of Famers Larry Bird and Kevin McHale, was the man in the middle for the Celtics as they won titles in 1980–81, 1983–84, and 1985–86.

When the Celtics began a rebuilding program in 1994–95, the rising Hornets were happy to take on a wise old hand. Parish provided stability as the backup center behind Alonzo Mourning. At the same time, in his nineteenth season, he continued to move up in the National Basketball Association record book. Parish is among the top ten career leaders in games played, minutes played, rebounds, blocked shots, and field goals.

Knicks
New York

The New York Knickerbockers were one of the National Basketball Association's original eleven franchises. And though the Knicks made the NBA finals three consecutive seasons, from 1951 through 1954, a championship eluded them for twenty-four seasons.

The breakthrough came in 1969–70 when a skilled cast of complementary players produced the regular season's best record, 60–22. Willis Reed was literally the center of attention, producing an average of 21.7 points and 13.9 rebounds per game. Walt Frazier ran the offense, finishing second in the league with an average of 8.2 assists per game and scoring 20.9 points per outing. The team also included Dave DeBusschere, Dick Barnett, future Chicago Bulls coach Phil Jackson, and future U.S. Senator Bill Bradley.

New York met the Los Angeles Lakers in the championship finals, but when Reed went down in Game Six with two severely stretched thigh muscles, Game Seven looked like a lock for the Lakers. Without the six-foot-ten-inch (208cm) center to guard him, Wilt Chamberlain had broken loose for 45 points and New York was blown out, 135–113. Still, the game was at Madison Square Garden, and when Reed announced he would play after a tentative pregame shooting session, the Knicks began to allow themselves hope.

It was Reed who scored the Knicks' first points on a shot from the top of the key. A minute later, Reed hit his second and last shot. Limping, he stayed in the game and played tenacious defense, limiting Chamberlain to just 2 baskets in 9 first-half shots. The Knicks led, 61–37, at the half, thanks to Reed's emotional play. The final was 113–99, and the Knicks had won their first championship.

Above: Bill Bradley attempts to get around future–Knick Head Coach Pat Riley. Below: Patrick Ewing salutes the crowd at Madison Square Garden after the Knicks' win over the Pacers in the seventh game of the Eastern Conference Semi-Finals. Opposite: Ewing takes the ball to the hoop versus Alonzo Mourning.

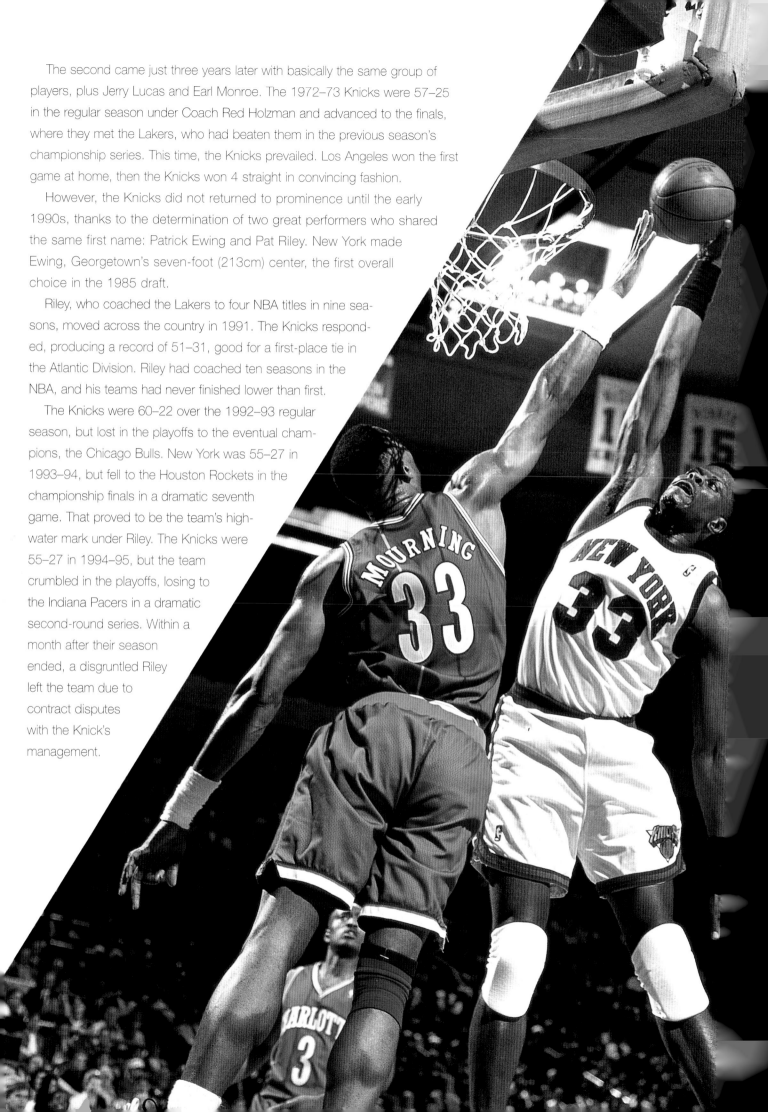

The second came just three years later with basically the same group of players, plus Jerry Lucas and Earl Monroe. The 1972–73 Knicks were 57–25 in the regular season under Coach Red Holzman and advanced to the finals, where they met the Lakers, who had beaten them in the previous season's championship series. This time, the Knicks prevailed. Los Angeles won the first game at home, then the Knicks won 4 straight in convincing fashion.

However, the Knicks did not returned to prominence until the early 1990s, thanks to the determination of two great performers who shared the same first name: Patrick Ewing and Pat Riley. New York made Ewing, Georgetown's seven-foot (213cm) center, the first overall choice in the 1985 draft.

Riley, who coached the Lakers to four NBA titles in nine seasons, moved across the country in 1991. The Knicks responded, producing a record of 51–31, good for a first-place tie in the Atlantic Division. Riley had coached ten seasons in the NBA, and his teams had never finished lower than first.

The Knicks were 60–22 over the 1992–93 regular season, but lost in the playoffs to the eventual champions, the Chicago Bulls. New York was 55–27 in 1993–94, but fell to the Houston Rockets in the championship finals in a dramatic seventh game. That proved to be the team's high-water mark under Riley. The Knicks were 55–27 in 1994–95, but the team crumbled in the playoffs, losing to the Indiana Pacers in a dramatic second-round series. Within a month after their season ended, a disgruntled Riley left the team due to contract disputes with the Knick's management.

Lakers
Los Angeles

There was a time when the hottest ticket in Los Angeles, maybe the world, was the Forum on a basketball night. When the Lakers played, it was known as Showtime, and it was beautiful to behold—unless you were rooting for the visiting team. Jack Nicholson and a glittering cast of celebrities watched through the 1980s as Kareem Abdul-Jabbar, Magic Johnson, James Worthy, Norm Nixon, and Michael Cooper elevated the game to an art.

In the 1980s, there was no team better; the Lakers won five of the decade's National Basketball Association championships. Overall, only the Celtics have won more than the Lakers' eleven franchise titles.

The fledgling league was a mere three years old when the Minneapolis Lakers were born in 1948. Their star was a bespectacled six-foot-ten-inch (208cm) center named George Mikan and he dominated the league, averaging 28.3 points per game. While seven-foot (213cm) players are commonplace today, Mikan was

The Lakers Win 33 Straight Games

Today's National Basketball Association schedules are a blur of walking through airports, watching soap operas in the hotel room, and playing in hostile arenas. Eighty-two games, stretched from autumn to spring, sometimes feel like an endless highway. Good teams win most of their games at home and do a little better than break even on the road. Bad teams? Don't ask.

Which brings us to the Los Angeles Lakers team of 1971–72. They were not merely a great team, they were the best regular-season team in NBA history. Between November 5, 1971, and January 7, 1972, they did not lose—not once. The Lakers won 33 straight games, an achievement that ranks with some of the greatest ever in professional sports.

That Lakers team was a marvelous mixture of talent: Wilt Chamberlain, Jerry West, Gail Goodrich, Elgin Baylor, Jim McMillian, and Pat Riley. The Lakers were 48–34, but nothing prepared the basketball world for what was about to unfold.

It began on November 5, when Los Angeles defeated the Baltimore Bullets, 110–106. The Lakers were playing with confidence, particularly on the defensive end, and they ripped through the rest of the month, winning 14 consecutive games. Media coverage of the team increased with every game.

"I played with the Globetrotters when they won 445 in a row," Chamberlain said, "and they were all on the road."

The Lakers met the Phoenix Suns, winners of 8 straight, on December 10. The Suns erased a 14-point fourth-quarter deficit to force overtime. Goodrich won it with 3 long-range jump shots. Los Angeles kept winning through the holiday season, smashing Atlanta 134–90 on January 7. That was the Lakers' thirty-third consecutive victory, and it turned out to be the last in the streak.

Led by Kareem Abdul-Jabbar, the Milwaukee Bucks put together an 18–2 run in the fourth quarter and won 120–104. The Lakers finished the season with a 69–13 record, a feat that has never been equaled. Fittingly, they cruised in the playoffs to the league championship.

Guard Jerry West fires over the Boston Celtics, the Lakers' greatest rivals.

head and shoulders taller than most opponents. The Lakers would set up Mikan under the basket and place his four teammates in a zone around the key.

Minneapolis won its first championship, defeating the Washington Capitals in the 1948–49 finals. The Lakers went on to win five titles in the six seasons between 1949 and 1954.

The franchise moved west to Los Angeles in 1960, but success stayed with the Lakers—it just took a little while to follow. The 1971–72 team almost redefined the word. Between November 5, 1971, and January 7, 1972, the Lakers did not lose a game. Guards Jerry West and Gail Goodrich provided most of the points while Wilt Chamberlain, hardly the dominant scoring force he was in Philadelphia, controlled the rebounds. One of the Lakers' reserve players was Pat Riley, who would one day coach the team.

The Lakers finished the season with a record of 69–13. Their final victory of the season came in the championship finals over the New York Knicks.

Los Angeles resurfaced at the top in 1979–80 when a six-foot-nine-inch (205cm) rookie guard named Earvin "Magic" Johnson left Michigan State University two years early. Johnson averaged 18 points, 7 rebounds, and 7 assists per game. And when the Lakers advanced to the championship finals opposite the Philadelphia 76ers, he played a new position—center. With Abdul-Jabbar unable to play because of a severely sprained ankle, Johnson guarded the 76ers' Darryl Dawkins. Johnson also produced 42 points, 15 rebounds, 7 assists, and 3 steals on offense to lead the Lakers to a 123–107 victory in Game Six.

With Johnson running the offense, Los Angeles would reach the finals eight times and come away with five championships.

In the nineties, after Johnson and Kareem retired, the team went through a rebuilding period. However, lead by Cedric Ceballos, the team made it to the second round of 1994–95 playoffs and showed that good things may still lie in store for the franchise.

Kareem Abdul-Jabbar shoots his patented skyhook over the 1986 Rockets' twintowers, Ralph Sampson and Hakeem Olajuwon.

Magic
Orlando

The cover of the Orlando Magic's 1994–95 media guide asks this presumptuous question: "Are you ready for this?" To back up the boast, there are action photographs of Shaquille O'Neal, Anfernee Hardaway, Horace Grant, Nick Anderson, and Dennis Scott.

Clearly, the Magic's future is now. But, believe it or not, the team existed before the arrival of Shaq. In fact, Orlando was born as an expansion franchise in time for the 1989–90 season. Their record that year was a dismal (but predictable) 18–64. The Magic had the worst defense in the National Basketball Association, averaging nearly 120 points allowed per game. There wasn't a single player listed among the league's significant statistical categories, maybe because an aging Reggie Theus and Terry Catledge were the team's two most talented players.

A dreadful 21–61 record in 1991–92 earned the Magic the right to pick first in the 1992 draft, and their general manager, Pat Williams, selected O'Neal, the seven-foot-one-inch (210cm), 303-pound (137 kg) center from Louisiana State University. Orlando immediately became a viable team. The Magic finished with a 41–41 record and was the league's most improved team under rookie head coach Brian Hill. O'Neal was the 1992–93 Rookie of the Year, based on his averages of 23.4 points, 13.9 rebounds, and 3.53 blocks per game.

Williams followed the choice of O'Neal with another draft-day coup. On June 30, 1993, Williams took Michigan's Chris Webber with the first overall choice, then dealt him to Golden State for Hardaway, who had been the third overall choice. The Warriors threw in three first-round draft choices, too. In a quiet way, Hardaway had a significant impact on the young team. He averaged 16 points, 6.6 assists, and 5.4 rebounds, falling just six votes shy of winning the Rookie of the Year Award, which ultimately went to Webber.

With O'Neal and Hardaway, the Magic finished the 1993–94 regular season with an impressive record of 50–32 and reached the playoffs for the first time in franchise history. Postseason play, however, is serious business. Orlando's lack of maturity was obvious in a 3-game sweep by the Indiana Pacers. And so, Williams went back to work.

Orlando needed more toughness on the boards and some playoff experience. The solution: Horace Grant of the Chicago Bulls. The six-foot-ten-inch (208cm) power forward owned three

Opposite, top: The Magic swarms for a rebound against the Bulls in the second round of the 1995 playoffs. Opposite, bottom: Hardaway gives Jordan a taste of his own medicine with a no-look pass. Left: The Kings just try to stay out of the way of this Shaq dunk.

championship rings and was a gritty rebounder who averaged 8.6 boards per game in seven seasons in Chicago. Williams signed Grant as a free agent in July 1994, and again, the Magic improved.

In March 1995, the Magic became the first team in the Eastern Conference to qualify for the playoffs. And then this team, having never won a playoff game, defeated Boston, Chicago, and Indiana in the playoffs before being swept by the more experienced Houston Rockets in the NBA finals.

Mavericks
Dallas

The Dallas Mavericks' first season in the National Basketball Association was predictably woeful. In 1980–81, the Mavericks' record was 15–67, placing them 37 games behind the San Antonio Spurs in the Midwest Division. They won only 4 of 41 road games, and not one player averaged more than 15 points per game.

In the gathering years, Dallas never made a big impression on the rest of the league. As the 1990s opened, the Mavs were a fairly wretched team. There is, however, an upside to consistently losing in the NBA: high draft choices.

And so, when Dallas finished with a record of 22–60 in 1991–92, they were able to take Ohio State guard Jimmy Jackson as the draft's fourth overall pick. When their record was 11–71 in 1992–93, the reward was University of Kentucky forward Jamal Mashburn, the fourth overall pick. And in 1993–94, when Dallas was 13–69, they obtained University of California point guard Jason Kidd, the second overall pick.

Sooner or later, that kind of talent had to start adding up in the victory column. As it turned out, 1994–95 was that year.

The Mavericks were a giddy 36–46 in the regular season and were actually in contention for the playoffs during the final month of the season, though they ultimately didn't make it. That marked an improvement of 23 wins from the previous season and underlined the high hopes of the organization for 1995–96 and beyond.

"Jason is not going to let his team lose very many games," says Head Coach Dick Motta. "I think between him and Jimmy and Jamal, we have some warriors who have so much pride that we're not going to get into the long losing streaks and stuff."

In many ways, Motta is the appropriate steady hand for this young team. Motta was 63 years old when he opened the 1994–95 season, his second stint with the Mavericks. Only Lenny Wilkens and Red Auerbach have more wins than Motta, who left the Mavericks in 1987 after differences with owner Donald Carter.

After failing to produce any substantial results in Sacramento, Motta returned to the team as a consultant in January 1994, while Quinn Buckner was still the team's head coach. After Buckner was fired, Motta was renamed coach, where he will most likely remain before turning the team over to rising assistant Brad Davis.

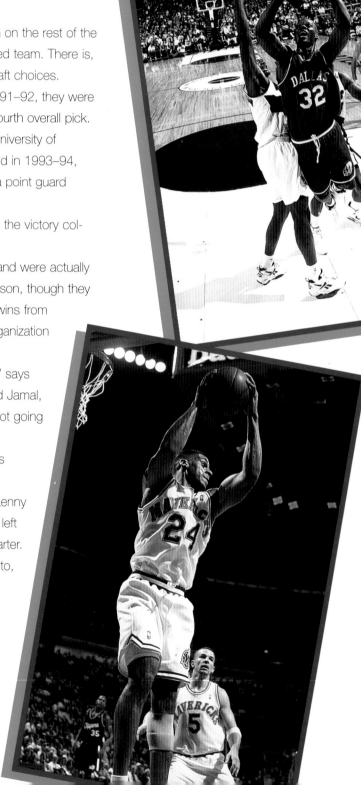

For Motta, an old-school coach, an adjustment was necessary.

"When I broadcasted Detroit Pistons games on TV I saw a lot of prima donnas meld to the point where winning was their main objective," Motta says. "[Coach] Chuck Daly was a mean son of a gun in college, but I watched him with the Pistons and he was half-loose. He never raised his voice to Isiah Thomas, yet they were playing hard. I said, 'Here's a guy who adjusted to the modern-day athlete.'

"That's basically what I decided to do here with these kids. It's that old saying of putting the velvet glove on the iron fist. Besides, I enjoy these kids. They're not out to take advantage of me. These guys are easy to be good to because they work."

Clearly, Motta's Mavericks are still a work in progress, but soon they could be one of the league's elite teams.

The dazzling trio of Jamal Mashburn (opposite, above), Jimmy Jackson (opposite, below), and Jason Kidd (right) makes the Dallas Mavericks a team to watch in the future.

Rockets
Houston

When the Houston Rockets joined the National Basketball Association for the 1971–72 season, there were no immediate fireworks. In truth, the Rockets fizzled to a record of 34–48, a staggering 35 games behind the Los Angeles Lakers.

The Rockets managed to reach the championship series twice, in 1981 and 1986, but Larry Bird and the Boston Celtics won both times in 6 games. But the 1993–94 Rockets had a greater sense of urgency and an extraordinarily great player. His name was Hakeem Olajuwon.

In his tenth year, the seven-foot (213cm) center had his best regular season ever. He averaged 27.3 points and 11.9 rebounds per game and was the league's Most Valuable Player. The playoffs, though, are another thing entirely. No one knew this better than Coach Rudy Tomjanovich, who played for Houston's inaugural team.

The 58–24 Rockets were a balanced team around Olajuwon: forwards Robert Horry and Otis Thorpe were solid rebounders and consistent scorers. The guards, Vernon Maxwell and Kenny Smith, were steady. Rookie guard Sam Cassell was a pleasant surprise off the bench.

Olajuwon, however, was the driving force. He scored 46 points in the second game of the Portland series. He added 37 more in the dramatic seventh game of the Phoenix series. His 41-point, 13-rebound effort in the second game of the Utah series was equally impressive.

By early June there were just two teams left: the Rockets and the New York Knicks. The 1994 championship series promised to be a battle of brutal, grinding defenses. Fans of offense would be disappointed.

Olajuwon ruined the Knicks' chances for victory in Game Six by blocking John Starks' three-point shot with 2 seconds left to preserve an 86–84 win for Houston. And so, appropriately, it came down to a seventh and final game.

The Rockets, playing in the comfort of the Summit, had history on their side: the last nineteen times an NBA playoff series had gone the distance, the home team had won. Make that twenty.

The Knicks' Starks was an unbelievable 2 for 18 from the field, including 0 for 11 from three-point range. Olajuwon produced 25 points, 10 rebounds, and 7 assists as Maxwell pumped in 21 points. Thus, the 90–84 victory gave Houston its first championship in franchise history. "This has to be considered a great team, and great teams are led by great players" then–Knicks Coach Pat Riley said. "Hakeem is a great player. This championship will kick him over the top."

For the first time since the introduction of the 24-second shot clock in 1954–55, neither team scored 100 points in any of the finals games. Houston set a seven-game championship series record by winning with only 603 points.

"If you write a book, you can't write it any better," Olajuwon said. "It has been a great season for us, and I'm so happy to bring a championship to this city."

In 1994–95 Olajuwon wrote an even better script. Underestimated as the sixth-seeded team in the Western Conference, Houston beat the four teams with the best regular-season records on its way to a second consecutive championship.

Inset: Anfernee Hardaway's shot and the Magic's championship hopes were knocked down by Hakeem Olajuwon. Left: Olajuwon puts up a shot against Shaq in Game Three of the 1995 finals.

Houston Rockets 89

Suns
Phoenix

The Phoenix Suns joined the National Basketball Association for the 1968–69 season. The result was a disastrous league-worst record of 16–66, 39 games behind the Los Angeles Lakers. Beyond a single appearance in the championship series in 1975–76 (they were beaten by the Boston Celtics), the Suns had not exactly burned brightly.

In the spring of 1992, the franchise made a conscious effort to change all that. They sent Jeff Hornacek, Andrew Lang, and Tim Perry to the Philadelphia 76ers in exchange for Charles Barkley, the colorful and controversial power forward. The return on the Suns' investment was startling and spectacular.

Under new head coach Paul Westphal, Barkley became the third player in league history to win the Most Valuable Player Award in the season immediately after being traded. His numbers: 25.6 points and 12.2 rebounds per game. The Suns were 62–20 in the 1992–93 regular season, a franchise record, and followed Barkley's lead all the way to the NBA finals.

Phoenix faced the Chicago Bulls, who were intent on winning their third consecutive championship. And though the Bulls were battered and bruised following their series win over the New York Knicks, the Suns were stunned in their own building, America West Arena. Phoenix became the first team in NBA finals history to lose the first 2 games at home. In those games, Chicago's Michael Jordan produced 73 points, 19 rebounds, 14 steals, and 7 steals.

"We're in a big hole right now, and we're in the right state for big holes," Barkley said. "We'd fit right into the Grand Canyon."

In the next game, the Suns responded with a terrific victory in triple overtime, 129–121, at Chicago Stadium. Six three-point baskets by Dan Majerle were the difference. Jordan scored 33 of his team's 61 first-half points in Game Four and the Bulls coasted to a 111–105 win. The Suns returned the favor in Game Five, 108–98, before Chicago, eventually closed out the series with a stirring 99–98 victory in Game Six.

Phoenix came back in 1993–94 with a 56–26 record, but injuries to Barkley and Kevin Johnson prevented the Suns from advancing as far in the playoffs as they had the previous year. Before the 1994–95 season, forwards Danny Manning and Wayman Tisdale turned down higher offers to sign with the Suns. Manning, who averaged 20.6 points a game in 1993–94, signed for a modest $1 million and a chance at a championship. Tisdale, who averaged 18.4 points and 7.2 rebounds for the Sacramento Kings over nearly six seasons, signed for a mere $850,000.

That gave Phoenix an enviable lineup that also included Majerle, A.C. Green, and Danny Ainge. It was Ainge who probably made the most important move of the off-season, persuading Barkley not to retire.

"It's Desert Storm," Johnson said, "We got all kinds of weapons." Even after Manning was lost for the season to reconstructive knee surgery, the Suns battled the San Antonio Spurs for the league's best record and finished three games behind with a mark of 59–23. Phoenix lost to Houston in the second round of the playoffs.

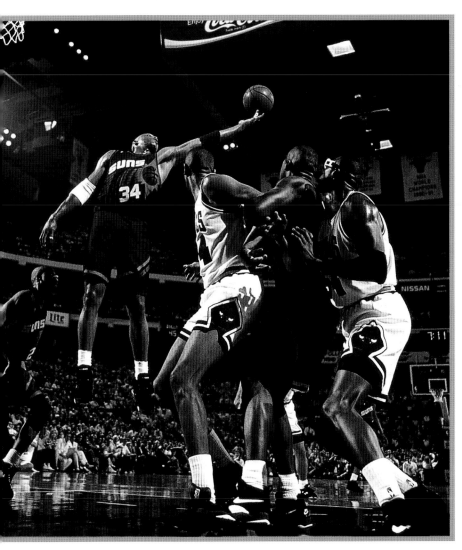

Opposite: Unfortunately for the Suns, Danny Manning did not soar in Phoenix during the 1994–95 season. Above: Charles Barkley was the prime mover in the Phoenix run to the 1993 NBA championship finals.

Mark West

Okay, it's quiz time: which active National Basketball Association player has the best shooting percentage? The answer is not Michael Jordan, Hakeem Olajuwon, Shaquille O'Neal, or Grant Hill. No, the most efficient shooter of today—and second on the all-time list to seven-foot-two-inch (218cm) center Artis Gilmore—is Mark West. Heading into the 1994–95 season, he had made 2,113 of 3,568 shots for a percentage of .592.

West was a solid player at Old Dominion University and was chosen in the second round of the 1983 draft by the Dallas Mavericks. After spending time in Milwaukee and Cleveland, the six-foot-ten-inch (208cm) center made a huge impression in Phoenix.

West was a rugged rebounder, but didn't score a ton of points. Still, he rarely took bad shots. In fact, he shot .653 in his first full season there, 1988–89. The next year, he led the NBA with a .625 mark and followed that with a .647 season.

The 1995 NBA Finals

In recent years an adage has developed around the National Basketball Association: you must lose and pay your dues before winning a championship.

Certainly, the Chicago Bulls learned that from the Detroit Pistons in 1989 and 1990. The Bulls and Michael Jordan lost to the Pistons in the 1989 Eastern Conference finals in six games and extended Detroit to seven games the next season. Thus steeled, Chicago won the next three NBA titles.

In 1995, the Orlando Magic challenged that conventional wisdom. With Shaquille O'Neal and Anfernee Hardaway playing at the top of their respective games, the Magic posted a 57–25 record. And then this team, which was in only its sixth season and had never won a playoff game, proceeded to march through the post season. They beat the tradition-rich Boston Celtics, ruined Jordan's comeback in a convincing series victory over Chicago, then vaulted into the NBA finals by eliminating Reggie Miller and the Indiana Pacers.

Though the Magic's opponent in the championship series, the Houston Rockets, were defending league champions, they were hardly overwhelming favorites. After defeating the New York Knicks to win the 1993–94 crown, the Rockets posted a pedestrian 47–35 record over the regular season. Houston was so desperate for a spark that they traded talented power forward Otis Thorpe to Portland for wiley guard Clyde Drexler.

The Rockets, seeded sixth in the Western Conference, had center Hakeem Olajuwon, whose 27.8-point scoring average was second only to O'Neal's 29.3, but apparently little else. And then the stuff of champions began to emerge.

Trailing the Utah Jazz (60–22 over the regular season) 2 games to 1, the Rockets rallied to win the series. Down to the Phoenix Suns (59–23) 3 games to 1, Houston prevailed again. The San Antonio Spurs (62–20) fell more easily. And so, the Rockets had beaten the league's three best teams without the benefit of

Hakeem Olajuwon was the essential difference in the Houston Rockets' second straight NBA championship.

a home-court advantage. Now they eyed the fourth, 57–25 Orlando.

While most experts conceded that Orlando had more ability, it was Houston, displaying muscular defense and versatile scoring, that prevailed with astonishing ease. In Game One, Olajuwon's tip of a Drexler miss with three-tenths of a second left in overtime gave the Rockets a 120–118 victory in Orlando. The Magic's Nick Anderson had missed 4 free throws in the last 10 seconds of regulation, which allowed the Rockets to force the game into overtime.

Game Two was a 117–106 victory for Houston as the Rockets set an NBA record with their seventh consecutive playoff road victory. Olajuwon had 34 points and guard Sam Cassell added 31. Olajuwon produced 31 points and 14 rebounds in a 106–103 win in Game Three, then pumped in 35 as the Rockets won Game Four 113–101 to sweep the series.

When the final tally was made, Olajuwon had scored 30 points or more in 16 of his 22 playoff games. He was the runaway choice for the series' Most Valuable Player. At the same time, the Rockets joined history's great title defenders: the Chicago Bulls, Detroit Pistons, Boston Celtics, and Los Angeles Lakers.

Hakeem Olajuwon, here shooting between Shaquille O'Neal and Horace Grant, collected the Most Valuable Player Award in the 1995 championship finals.

The Basketball Hall of Fame

There is a place where Magic Johnson still makes the unbelievable no-look pass, where Larry Bird still hoists the perfect three-point shot, where Julius Erving still floats through the lane with the greatest of ease.

All these things and much more can be found at the Basketball Hall of Fame in Springfield, Massachusetts, the birthplace of basketball. More than a century after Dr. James Naismith invented the game, it is preserved and celebrated here with love.

The game's great players are all captured in bronze and their great feats detailed in the Honors Court. There are uniforms of the stars, from high school to college to the National Basketball Association. There is the jersey worn by Kareem Abdul-Jabbar when he carried the Los Angeles Lakers to championship after championship. There is the sneaker—size 22—that belonged to Bob Lanier when he played for the Detroit Pistons.

Visitors are invited to play the game, too. You can test your skill at the free throw line and three-point field goals, and you can see if your vertical leap measures up to Shaquille O'Neal's.

There are television monitors at every turn, playing highlights from recent National Collegiate Athletic Conference championship games and offering great moments from the Olympics. The game's best coaches can also be found on exhibit.

The Basketball Hall of Fame has something for everyone.

Photography Credits

Index